CAPTURING READERS WITH CHILDREN'S CHOICE BOOK AWARDS

A Directory of State Programs

CHILDREN'S CHOICE AWARDS

BEVERLY J. OBERT AND PATTY BARR

Linworth
PUBLISHING, INC

Your Trusted
Library-to-Classroom Connection.
Books, Magazines, and Online.

To all the school and public librarians who introduce children and young adults to the world of literature through children's choice book awards.

Cataloging-in-Publication Data

Obert, Beverly J.
  Capturing readers with children's choice book awards : a directory of state programs / Beverly J. Obert and Patty Barr.
      p. cm.
  Includes bibliographical references and index.
  ISBN 1-58683-169-0 (pbk.)
  1. Children's literature—Awards—United States—Directories. 2. Young adult literature—Awards—United States—Directories. 3. Children—Books and reading—United States. 4. Teenagers—Books and reading—United States. 5. Reading promotion—United States 6. Children's literature—Bibliography. 7. Young adult literature—Bibliography. I. Barr, Patty. II. Title.
  Z1037.A2O24 2004
  028.5'5'0973—dc22

                                            2004012671

Author: Beverly J. Obert and Patty Barr

Linworth Books:
Carol Simpson, Editorial Director
Donna Miller, Editor
Judi Repman, Associate Editor

Published by Linworth Publishing, Inc.
480 East Wilson Bridge Road, Suite L
Worthington, Ohio 43085

Copyright © 2004 by Linworth Publishing, Inc.

ISBN: 1-58683-169-0

5 4 3 2 1

Table of Contents ⸺⸺⸺⸺⸺

Table of Contents continued ___

Table of Contents continued _____

Table of Figures _____

Introduction

Children's choice awards are exciting and fun. A successful award program takes dedication, but for most involved it is a labor of love; a love of books, reading, and introducing children to the pleasures of reading. While children's choice awards have been in existence for many years, the literature is sparse about why they were created, who sponsors them, and how books are selected for the lists.

This book is intended as a complete listing of all the various children's choice awards in the United States. Only those awards are included in which students, grades kindergarten through high school, read and vote on the awards. Chapter one contains a brief history of children's choice awards, the first awards, how awards have developed through the years, an overview of the steering committee structure, methods for selecting books, voting criteria, and development of award names and logos.

The second chapter provides tips for preparing to participate in a children's choice program. This chapter will be especially helpful to the new teacher or librarian who has never been involved in such a program, but seasoned teachers and librarians will also find some useful, new ideas to use.

The third chapter contains the listing of states and awards. Included for each award are the year of the first award, official Web sites, grade levels, sponsors, purpose, how the name was determined, criteria for how books are chosen for the list, and criteria for student voting. Award-winning books are listed chronologically. The appendix contains a chronological listing of the awards. A bibliography and indices with authors, illustrators, and titles complete the book.

This book is designed for school librarians and teachers serving kindergarten through twelfth grades. It will be helpful to those who have previously implemented a children's choice award program as well as those just getting started. Public librarians will find this book useful as a guide for promoting state awards. Both school and public librarians can use the award information as a collection development tool to find books that are popular with students. Instructors at colleges and universities who teach children's literature classes should find this book a useful resource. These lists of award-winning books will help librarians make creative displays.

Acknowledgements

T he authors wish to thank all of the members of the various state committees who worked with us to make sure that the information for their state award was accurate and for giving us permission to include their state award and logos in this book.

Thanks to the Rolling Prairie Library System, Decatur, Illinois for their support. Having a quiet place to work after hours allowed us to work more productively.

Thanks go to the Illinois library community who supported and encouraged us during the process of planning and writing this book.

Thanks to Doris McKay, consultant at Rolling Prairie Library System, for her expertise in developing an Access database that allowed us to more easily compile all of this information. Thanks also to Rolling Prairie staff members, Peggy Durst for her proofreading skills and Jo McLain for her computer graphic expertise.

Thanks to Donna Miller and Sherry York of Linworth Publishing, Inc. for giving us the opportunity to author a book and for their encouragement and help along the way.

Finally thanks to our families for their support and understanding when meals were not made and laundry was left undone.

About the Authors

M s. Obert holds a BA in music education from Western Illinois University, Macomb, Illinois and an MSLIS from the University of Illinois Urbana-Champaign. She has been a teacher of music, a public library director, and since 1994 has been a consultant with the Rolling Prairie Library System based in Decatur, Illinois. She is an active member of the Illinois Library Association and the Illinois School Library Media Association. Her knowledge of children's choice awards is first hand as a member of the *Rebecca Caudill Young Readers' Book Award* Steering Committee since 1994, where she coordinates and edits an activity pack for the list of 20 nominated titles.

Mrs. Barr's BS degree in early childhood education, and her MS in library and information science are from the University of Illinois in Urbana-Champaign. She has been a school librarian for 12 years, currently serving students in grades PreK-4 in Monticello, Illinois. She has worked for BabyTALK, a family literacy program, since 1989, and has served on the *Rebecca Caudill Young Readers' Book Award* as a reader/evaluator for six years.

A History of
Children's Choice
Book Awards

C hildren's choice awards are those state book awards in which the students nominate, read, and vote for their favorite book. They have a long history, which goes back more than 50 years. The first award established as a children's choice award was the *Young Reader's Choice Award* by the Pacific Northwest Library Association, a regional award for northwestern United States and Canada.

The first state to establish an individual award was Kansas. That award was the *William Allen White Children's Book Award*, established in 1952 by Ruth Garver Gagliardo at Emporia State University in Kansas. The award was named after a distinguished citizen of Kansas who wished to encourage boys and girls of Kansas to read and enjoy good books. The first award was given in 1953 for *Amos Fortune, Free Man*, written by Elizabeth Yates (Dutton, 1950).

The second individual state award began in 1956 in Vermont, and was named the *Dorothy Canfield Fisher Award*. Ms. Fisher was an author and educator who lived and worked in Vermont. Established by the Vermont PTA and the Vermont Department of Libraries, the award's purpose is "to help children become enthusiastic and discriminating readers." The first award was given in 1957 to Mildred Mastin Pace, author of *Old Bones, the Wonder Horse* (McGraw-Hill, 1955).

In the years between the late fifties and the early eighties several additional states created children's choice book awards targeted to grades four through eight. These awards were created primarily for the purpose of promoting literature to children. From the mid-eighties to the early nineties the number of children's choice awards grew. The *Rebecca Caudill Young Readers' Book Award* in Illinois is one such award. This award, created by the Illinois School Library Media Association, the Illinois Reading Council, and the Illinois Association of Teachers of English, shows a pattern followed by many of the awards created during this time period. Various library associations, reading councils, or public libraries banded together to establish book awards. Committees were formed consisting of members from each association. The membership of the committee is often lengthy, lasting for many years, or changing on a rotating basis of one to three years.

The committees that oversee the awards are structured in a variety of ways. Many states follow a similar pattern of having one core committee that oversees the award with subcommittees working on such activities as nominations, reading, and evaluating.

The *Nevada Young Readers' Award (NYRA)* is an interest group of the Nevada Library Association. Members of the *NYRA* vote for a chairperson and a chairperson-elect. The chairperson serves for one year, not to exceed two consecutive terms, and has an extensive list of duties spelled out in the rules and procedures. The chair must facilitate all communications of the group, schedule business meetings, submit a budget, work with publishers, edit and publish booklets, and can appoint committees to carry out the functions of the interest group. The chairperson-elect assists with the functions designated by the chairperson.

Wyoming's *Soaring Eagle* committee is made up of eight members, four from each sponsoring organization, appointed by governing members of the organizations. The members serve three-year terms with not more than half the committee represented by new members each year. Two members act as co-chairs, one from each organization, and are responsible to the parent organization. Their terms of office expire on alternating years. Members must be on the committee for at least one year before becoming a chairperson.

The *Rebecca Caudill Young Readers' Book Award* in Illinois has a steering committee made up of a chairperson, two members appointed from each of the sponsoring organizations, two members representing public libraries, two members representing library systems, and one member from the academic community. The committee meets two times per year in September and January. Subcommittees consist of Award Committee, Packet Committee, Publicity Committee, Evaluator's Committee, Records and Registration Committee, *Let's Talk About Books* Committee, as well as a secretary, treasurer, and the chairperson. There are no set terms for the members.

The *Eliot Rosewater Indiana High School Book Award* Committee (*Rosie* Committee) has a maximum of thirty voting members and one ex-officio (nonvoting) member, who is the president of the Association for Indiana Media Educators (AIME). Terms are for two years and may be renewed. All adult members shall be members of AIME and two thirds of the adult members must be high school library media specialists. The committee also has student members with many of the same responsibilities as the adult members. The students must attend the book selection meeting, read the books being considered for nomination, participate in the *Rosie* listserv, monitor the committee Web site and assist the library media specialists in promoting the *Rosie* program. The adult members have additional responsibilities of attending organizational and book selection meetings, assisting the chair with promoting and publicizing the program, fund-raising, recruiting student committee members, and if possible, attending the *Rosie Award* presentation.

From the early nineties to the present, the trend is for states to change grade levels for established awards. It is common to see a grade four-to-eight award separated into four-to-six and six-to-eight awards. An example of this separation is the *William Allen White Children's Book Award,* which was for grades three to eight. In 2001, two awards were given: one for grades three to five and a second for grades six to eight.

Another trend is the creation of picture book and high school awards. These awards also require: the submission of possible titles with specific criteria; reading and evaluation; selection of a list; and promotion of books to the students, who then read and vote for their favorite book. New awards are being established. Iowa has a new high school award with the first winner announced in 2004. In Illinois, a new kindergarten to third grade award, the *Monarch Award*, and the *Abraham Lincoln Illinois High School Book Award* are being established to join the original fourth through eighth grade *Rebecca Caudill* award.

In Delaware there are two awards for the same age group of children, the *Delaware Blue Hen Book Award* (K-8), which begins a teen award for 2005, and the *Delaware Diamonds Primary Award* (K-5). The two committees of the awards have begun talks that may result in the merging of the awards. This merger seems most appropriate so that the best of both awards can be brought together, giving the children of Delaware a richer literary experience.

What types of books receive these awards? Fiction books lead the list of books that win children's choice awards. However, several states have awards for other categories of books. Utah has informational and poetry book awards, and New Jersey has a chapter book award as well as nonfiction awards for both younger and older students.

While most awards are for only one state, one regional award, the *Young Reader's Choice Award*, is sponsored by the Pacific Northwest Library Association. Students in fourth through twelfth grades take part in this award in the states of Washington, Oregon, Alaska, Idaho, Montana, and the Canadian provinces of British Columbia and Alberta. Their first award was given in 1940 for *Paul Bunyan Swings His Axe* by Dell J. McCormick

(Caxton Printers Ltd., 1936). The idea for the award came in 1938 from Seattle bookseller Harry Hartman. Hartman wrote, "For quite a number of years we have wished that each year some recognition would be given to a book for children which young readers endorse as being an excellent story. The reading habit is best developed through reading those books which are most entertaining and instructive from the young person's point of view." *Handbook for the Young Reader's Choice Nominees* by Bette D. Ammon and Gale W. Sherman (Pocatello, Idaho: Beyond Basals, 1900s-).

A national children's choice award was established by The Writer's Conference, Inc., a nonprofit organization in Overland, Kansas. *The Heartland Award for Excellence in Young Adult Literature* began in 1996 with a threefold purpose: to encourage the participation of young adults in the reading of young adult literature, to encourage the teaching of this literature in middle and secondary schools as supplemental and in-class reading, and to aid in the goal that all young adults become lifelong readers.

Any young adult literature enthusiast may submit nominations for the master list of ten books. Students in grades six through twelve who read at least three of the books are eligible to vote for their favorite. The winning author is invited to a literature festival at the University of Kansas in the fall.

The winner of the 2003 *Heartland Award* was *The Sisterhood of the Traveling Pants* by Ann Brashares (Delacorte, 2001). Information about nominations and voting can be found at the award's Web site at <www.writingconference.com/heartlan.htm>.

Missouri, in addition to sponsoring *The Show Me Readers Award, The Mark Twain Award*, and *The Gateway Award* for grades one through twelve, also encourages children from birth to kindergarten to listen to and vote for their favorite picture book. *The Missouri Building Block Picture Book Award* began in 1996 and is administered by the Children's Services Round Table of the Missouri Library Association. Preschool children who listen to a minimum of five of the ten nominated books may vote for their favorite. Public libraries primarily promote and facilitate this award.

The 2003 winner of the *Building Block Award* was *"Who Took the Cookies From the Cookie Jar?"*, by Bonnie Lass and Philemon Sturges (Little, Brown, 2000). More information can be found on their Web site at <http://molib.org/BuildingBlock.html>.

Award names can be divided into four categories. First are those who simply put their state name in front of the words "Children's Book Award" or "Young Readers' Award". The purpose of the award is immediately apparent. Other states become a bit more creative and use the state nickname (New Mexico's *Land of Enchantment Book Award)*; state landmark, (New Hampshire's *Great Stone Face Award)*; state flower, (Texas *Bluebonnet Award)*; or the state mammal, (North Dakota's *Flicker Tale Children's Book Award)*.

Some awards are named for people. In Illinois, the *Rebecca Caudill Young Readers' Book Award* is named for an author of children's books who lived and wrote in Illinois. Children's authors are the most common names, but others who have been honored include educators (*Patricia Gallagher Award* in Oregon), famous citizens (*William Allen White Award* in Kansas), or fictional characters in books (Indiana *Rosie Award* for the name of a character in one of Kurt Vonnegut's books).

The final category includes miscellaneous names that begin with a state symbol. As the awards have split into more grade levels, names have been selected with related themes. Wyoming is an example with *Buckaroo*, *Indian Paintbrush*, and *Soaring Eagle* awards. South Dakota has the *Prairie Bud* and *Prairie Pasque* awards, two different awards named after the blooming stages of the state flower.

How do books make the reading list? Each state has set a criteria and procedure for the selection of books. First, the books must be nominated. Students are encouraged to nominate books, but librarians, teachers, and parents also nominate books. In some states there is a copyright restriction. At the time of nomination, a book must have been published within two to five years of the nomination. Nominated books must often meet additional criteria. Some states require books be published in the United States, some states allow translations, and others do not. Universally, textbooks are excluded from the nominations and generally books from a series, such as *The Baby-Sitters Club,* are not eligible. Award winners such as the Newbery and Caldecott are often excluded. Another criterion requires that the author be living for their book to be considered.

Once the books are nominated, a committee evaluates the nominations and compiles a list of possible titles. These titles are then read by committee members and evaluated for their literary quality and child appeal. At some point, the readers meet and vote for their favorite books, bringing the list down to approximately five to twenty-five books that are found on the final list. The selection meeting is often very interesting with diverse views, strong opinions, and a lively exchange of ideas. When the final list is set, it is announced to students.

Just how does the above process work? Examples from a few states illustrate the process. In Illinois, the evaluators' committee receives nominations only on the official nomination form. The nominations are reviewed and many are eliminated because they do not meet the criteria. A small nominations subcommittee of approximately five members then reviews the remaining titles, reducing the number to 100. The 100 titles selected are chosen based on the number of nominations received, appropriateness to the grade level of the award, and reviews. If more than one book by an author is nominated, the subcommittee determines which title will be added to the list. The list of 100 books is arranged alphabetically by the author's last name and mailed to approximately 70 readers. They have less than three months to read 10 of the titles, evaluate them using an evaluation instrument based on a point scale, and return the evaluations to the chair of the evaluators' committee. The eight criteria of the evaluation instrument are as follows:

1. Literary quality (evaluates the style, tone, and voice of the author)

2. Qualities of originality, imagination, and vitality in text and illustration (evaluates the book as a whole including text, illustrations, and edition)

3. Element of timelessness (evaluates the lasting interest and quality of the book)

4. Clarity and readability (evaluates the overall organization and flow of the text)

5. Appropriate in subject, treatment, and format to the age group of grades four through eight for which the award is intended

6. Theme and subject matter of value to children and young people

7. The likelihood of acceptance by children and young people

8. Factual accuracy (should be given 10 points in every case, unless there is a factual inaccuracy in a nonfiction book, or an inaccuracy in a fiction book that detracts from the overall quality of the work)

The reader rates the book giving a point value from one to ten on each of the criteria. The highest number of points a book can receive is 80. The evaluator chair arranges the titles by point totals, and the 50 titles with the highest number of points advance. The 70 readers are mailed the full list of 50, and they read as many as they can between the first of October and the first of February. An all-day meeting is held in February with all the readers and the steering committee. Each of the 50 books is discussed and voted on. Those present do not vote for any book that they have not read. Titles with a tally difference of 10 votes or less are tabled until the end of the day. After all 50 books have been voted on, if any of the 20 slots on the list are open, the tabled books are again reviewed. If there are five tabled books and two slots are open, each person present has two votes and must decide which of the five titles will get their vote. The two books that receive the highest votes fill the final slots on the list.

The process for the Vermont *Red Clover Award* is different. The committee looks at all the picture books published in just one year. The eligibility requirements reduce that number to approximately 500 titles. Each committee member reads as many books as possible and exchanges recommendations. They meet over the Christmas holidays and begin making

FIGURE 1.1: Kentucky Bluegrass Award Ballot

KENTCKY BLUEGRASS AWARD BALLOT

Title of book: _____

Mark One Box	😃 It's Great!	🙂 It's Good.	😐 It's Okay.	🙁 It's not too bad.	😞 It's bad.

Comments:

_____

_____

_____

Is this the first book you've read from this year's KBA list?   Yes   No

Do you plan to read more books from this year's KBA list?   Yes   No

Are you a (circle one)?   BOY   GIRL

What grade are you in? _____

KENTCKY BLUEGRASS AWARD BALLOT

Title of book: _____

Mark One Box:	Comments:
👍👍👍👍👍 It's Great!	
👍👍👍👍 It's Good.	
👍👍👍 It's Okay.	
👍👍 It's not too bad.	
It's Bad.	

Is this the first book you've read from this year's KBA list?   Yes   No
Do you plan to read more books from this year's KBA list?   Yes   No
Are you a (circle one)?   MALE   FEMALE
What grade are you in? _____

recommendations of favorite books. By their February selection meeting, a shorter list of approximately 30 books is presented for serious discussion. Members take turns presenting books, discussing the strengths and weaknesses, and then voting. By the end of the day a list of 10 titles has made the list. During that day each book is carefully examined for its own quality and for the list balance as a whole. This two-day process is just the start for the committee as they also develop a manual, present books at the Vermont Library Conference, have a business meeting where plans for the *Red Clover* Conference are made, and attend the *Red Clover* Conference.

Participation by schools and public libraries in a children's choice award is voluntary. Each school decides if it wishes to participate and then registers with the award program. Not all grades in a school have to be included. Public libraries often participate in the programs, working with private schools and home schoolers to offer those students the opportunity to vote for their favorite books. Once registered, the school or library receives information about the books on the list, ballots, posters, and order forms for bookmarks and other promotional items. Many states have packets that contain information about the authors, questions for discussion, book talks, and more to aid the busy librarian in implementing the program.

Voting usually takes place in the spring from late February to May. Schools decide when and how the children will vote. The number of books the children must read to be able to vote varies from state to state. If there are few books on the list, they must read all of the books to be eligible to vote. With a list of 10 or more, the requirement is to read two to five books. A book read to the students by a teacher in the classroom also counts for voting eligibility. Most awards allow the children to vote only once. In Kentucky, however, the students vote for each book they read, ranking it as "It's Great, It's Good, It's Okay, It's Not Too Bad, or It's Bad." There are two forms of the ballot; one with smiley faces and one with thumbs-up.

The Colorado ballot is unique as it serves a double purpose as ballot and nomination form. Most ballots are a simple listing of the books followed by a short line to mark the favorite. The total of all votes cast at a school are sent to the committee and tallied. The book with the most votes wins the award.

The newest wrinkle in children's book awards is the Internet. Many awards have their own Web sites. These sites vary in depth of coverage, currency, and accuracy of information. As this book was written, the authors relied heavily on the Web sites for initial information about the awards. Some are well designed and full of detail. These sites are easy to navigate and have complete coverage.

Kansas: *William Allen White Children's Book Award*
<www.emporia.edu/libsv/wawbookaward/>

Nebraska: *The Golden Sower Award*
<www.nol.org/home/NLA/golden/sower.htm>

Illinois: *Rebecca Caudill Young Readers' Book Award*
<www.rcyrba.org>

Wisconsin: *The Golden Archer Award*
<www.wemaonline.org/cm.archer.cfm>

The book awards have many different logos. The logos for awards generally follow the name of the award. Those named for a person have the likeness of the person as the logo. The outline of the state are often found as one component of the logo along with the name. There are a wide variety, from simple letter schemes to medallions. Most of the logos can be located on the award Web sites.

A few interesting statistics about children's choice awards show that awards exist in 49 of the 50 states. Mississippi has no award program. One thousand twenty-five books have been honored through the awards programs. Beverly Cleary has won the most awards; 18 of her books have won awards across the country. Kate DiCamillo's book, *Because of Winn-Dixie*, is the individual book with the most awards, with 28 states honoring her novel. Close behind are *Superfudge* by Judy Blume, with 27 awards, and *Holes* by Louis Sachar, with 26 awards.

Children's choice awards exist because of dedicated volunteers who believe that these awards will encourage children to read and become more literate citizens. They will continue to grow and expand to encompass many age groups and genres.

IMPLEMENTING
THE PROGRAM

CHAPTER

2

Enthusiasm is the most important facet of starting a children's choice program in a school or library. A library can own multiple copies of the books on the list, but without someone to promote the program, those books might gather dust on the shelves. Most children's choice award programs exist to promote reading for enjoyment, not to promote competition among readers. Think about your reasons for joining a children's choice program before deciding to participate.

Planning

When first beginning participation in a state award program, look at the award Web site. Most of the information needed can be found there, including the rules for participation, how to register and send in vote tallies, a list of the nominated books, and information about how to run an award program. Another first step is to visit and talk with a librarian near you who has been involved in an award program.

The cooperation of administrators and teachers is a vital step to making the children's choice award successful. Sometimes these programs require extra funding, which may need to be approved by an administrator. Involve them by enthusiastically promoting the award. Explain the purpose of the award, give a history and outline of how you plan to implement the program, and detail the costs to be incurred. Involve the teachers by giving a short PowerPoint presentation about the award books at a faculty meeting. Emphasize that reading scores could improve with the students' involvement in the award program. Mention that students take a special pride in reading and voting for books in a program designed just for them. Point out that many of the books are appropriate for teachers to use as a read-aloud in the classroom. Quite a few of the states have activity packets that accompany the list. Share these with the teachers, or offer to help them develop their own.

It is important that the program coordinator, usually the library media specialist, acquires books that fit the reading and interest levels of the students at their particular school. For example, if the award is voted on by students in grades four through eight, and the building is kindergarten through fourth, consideration should be given as to whether purchasing books at the seventh and eighth grade level would be appropriate. Conversely, books on a lower reading level may not be challenging enough for older readers. The wise librarian reads all of the books on the list or at least reads the reviews to determine appropriateness for their students. Multiple copies of the books are needed so the students can meet the program requirements.

Cash-strapped school districts may not provide funding for the library media specialist to purchase multiple copies of books. Mini-grants from parent organizations are a funding source to investigate. Would a business buy a classroom set of books? Check the price of a set of paperbacks and present a civic club with the opportunity to make a difference by purchasing a complete set. Many book clubs and book fairs include copies of the books at reduced prices. Another idea is to hold a read-a-thon to raise money for books. Invite prominent members from the community to read aloud during the read-a-thon.

The program coordinator should create a time line to organize the activities and events of the program. Administrative organization helps the program run efficiently. Items to include in your time line include the following:

- Register for the program and acquire book list (May)
- Order, catalog, and process books (May through September)
- Plan promotional activities
- Promote program and books to teachers and staff (September)
- Introduce books to students (October)
- Conduct activities (October through the voting)
- Conduct the voting (Usually mid-February through April 1)
- Post local winners
- Report voting results to award committee
- Award nomination deadline
- Announce state winner

The suggested time frame assumes a program with the vote tally due to the committee in late February or March. If the award in your state has a different time frame, you will have to adjust accordingly.

Register to participate in the award program as early as possible to ensure the receipt of any materials necessary for the smooth implementation of the program. Also, the earlier the registration, the sooner the planning can take place. Many programs have a small registration fee, and some provide for online registration. Extra promotional materials, such as mugs, activity packets, pencils, T-shirts, and other prizes are available at a low cost in some states. Early registration allows more time to solicit funds for books or promotional materials.

Once the books arrive, process and distribute them in a timely fashion for student use. Marking the books with stickers or other identification will help the children to easily locate the books. Stickers with the award logo on them can be purchased from many award committees. Placing the books on a special shelf or display area is even better. Posters or lists of the books displayed in strategic spots around the library and school will help to promote them as well.

Decide on activities to promote the books. Many resources are available to help determine what activities will be most useful. Introduce the books to teachers and students as the first activity. Booktalking the books on the list is the best way for teachers and students to learn about the books. Spreading the other activities out over the course of the program will maintain student interest. Involve other staff members in these activities whenever possible. With the support of the staff, the program will be successful.

Checklist of Promotional Activities

- Book displays
- Bookmarks:
    List of all the books
    Individual books
- Author visits
- Bulletin boards:
    Book covers
    Authors
    Genres
    Time line
    Map the location of the books' settings
- Booktalks
- Reading books aloud to students
- Book clubs/book discussion groups
- Student or library newsletter articles

- Contests:
    - Bookmark
    - Poster
    - New book cover
    - T-shirt

Booktalking is the best way to introduce the books to the teachers and students. Many books and Web sites on booktalking are available. These resources contain actual booktalks you can use. Activity packets with booktalks for the current award book list are available from many award programs. The selected bibliography at the end of this book contains suggested books and Web sites for the novice booktalker to use.

Students can read or listen to books on the list to be eligible to vote. Encourage teachers to read aloud to students. Tips for reading aloud include the following:

- Read the book beforehand so that you are comfortable reading the content aloud.
- Look up unfamiliar words to pronounce them correctly.
- Decide how you will pronounce names of characters and be consistent.
- If phrases or words are in another language, ask for help with the pronunciation.
- Read with enthusiasm, changing the pace and volume of your speech to match the action.
- You do not have to read with different voices, but read clearly and with pauses so that the listener can distinguish between characters.
- If the book is illustrated, show the illustrations to the listeners.

Electronic Reading Programs

Electronic reading programs such as Accelerated Reader (AR) and Reading Counts (RC) are found in many schools throughout the United States. When used with a children's choice award program, electronic reading programs have an advantage; recordkeeping is simplified. Children read the book, take a test, and the results are posted and kept track of by a computer. These electronic programs simplify the task of tracking which and how many books each student has read.

If your school uses one of these electronic reading programs, follow these suggestions. When ordering the books for the children's choice program, check to see if you have the test for these books. If the test is not owned, investigate the option of ordering a customized test disk. A customized disk contains only the tests that are requested and most companies offer this option. An alternative to purchasing a disk is to create tests for books. Both AR and RC allow you to create tests. Enlist the help of teachers in the school to create the tests. Depending on the size of the school, each teacher might read from one to four books and create tests for them. Select those teachers who support the children's choice award program and encourage their students to read the books. Teachers could read the books during the summer to gain a head start on the year.

Advanced readers in the upper grades can also create tests. They can read the books and create tests under the supervision of a teacher. Develop guidelines for writing the test questions, such as one question per chapter or one question about the main character or setting of the book. Because some of the books on the award list may be ranked below the reading level of more advanced students, having them read and create tests expands their experience with the lower-level books.

Gaining the approval of teachers to allow students to read all of the award books, no matter what the reading level, is a hurdle, librarians must overcome. Because the book awards cover multiple grades, multiple levels of reading are available. Schools or teachers that rigidly enforce each student's reading level will find it difficult to participate in a children's choice book award program.

For example, a student in the eighth grade may have to read books at a level of 8.2, but if most of the books on the master list are at a 5.0 to 6.2 level or below, the student is not able to participate in the award program because the books are not "at their reading level." Even when a teacher says the student can read the lower-level books, in actuality, students only read books that give them the reading points needed for completion of their AR or RC goals.

Encouraging teachers with rigid requirements to buy into the award program is difficult but not impossible. Limit the time that the program runs to one or two months to encourage teachers to be flexible in allowing students to read below their reading level. The drawback is that students may not have time to read the required number of books to be eligible to vote for their favorite.

Another approach is to work with the coordinator of the electronic reading program. Many schools have one person who coordinates the program, gathering input from the teachers on what they feel the required number of points or pages read should be at each grade level and how far above or below reading level students may read when a book captures their interest. Once the input is gathered, the coordinator compiles and prepares a recommendation to the staff. By approaching the use of the electronic program this way, there is a logical progression in what students are required to do at each grade level. This strategy also ensures that each class in a grade level is working on the same requirements. Contact the coordinator when thinking of starting a children's choice program and discuss the benefits students will gain from participating in the program, the reading levels of books on the master list, and how best to integrate the children's choice program into the electronic reading program. Collaborate in determining how best to introduce the program to the teachers in order to gain teacher support and active involvement in the award program.

If your school has no coordinator, the job is a bit harder. First, learn the requirements set by each of the teachers. If the requirements are very rigid or high, you may decide to start the program with one grade level or with those teachers whose requirements most closely match the reading level of the books on the master list. However, if the requirements are flexible, take the idea of beginning this program to a teachers' meeting. Not all teachers will choose to participate, but that is okay. It is better to start small with a few enthusiastic teachers. Once students have read the books and voted, they will want to participate the next year. That is the time to approach the teachers at that next grade level, getting them on board to implement the children's choice program in their classes.

The use of electronic reading programs with children's choice awards is possible. Careful selection of an approachable teacher, the books to be read, and planning will lead to a successful program with students reading enthusiastically.

Recordkeeping and Voting

It is important to have an accurate recordkeeping device because many award programs require students to read a certain number of books on the list before voting. A wall chart with stickers, short reports on note cards, Accelerated Reader or other electronic tests, or one-on-one book conferences with the teacher or librarian are ways to keep track of what has been read. The key is to find a system that is easy to implement, that students can do themselves, and that will encourage healthy competition.

Possible Recording Methods

- Four by six card file: Place the student's name at the top of the card with the books read recorded beneath it
- Computerized spreadsheet
- Three-dimensional graphic: For example, create a tree and for each book read add a leaf
- Three-ring binder with pages for individual students
- File folders: For each class or each student
- Accelerated Reader/Reading Counts test results
- Wall charts for each class

Build excitement as voting day approaches. Have students run an "election" campaign, making posters or giving speeches to sway voters to their choice. Hold a countdown to voting day through school announcements to let students know how many days they have left to read a book or sway a vote. Some other possible pre-voting day activities include the following:

- Make a television or radio commercial for the books
- Interview characters from the books
- Dress up like a favorite character from a book on the list
- Present a campaign speech
- Make a campaign poster
- Design an advertisement
- Design a button or business card for the books

Any of the above activities that can be taped should be. The recordings can then be played over the school's public address or video system. They may also be appropriate for showing on the local cable channel. If showing students on the public access channels, permission must be obtained from parents or guardians.

The actual voting method depends on how many children are involved. Small groups may meet in the library at lunch on voting day, vote, and share a special decorated cake. Another option is student discussion of their favorite books followed by the marking of their ballots. Larger groups of children may have to take turns voting, possibly in simulated voting booths or online in computer labs. Possible voting methods include the following:

- Online voting
- Paper ballot
- Punch tab ballot and borrowed voting machines
- Raise hands
- Boxes for each book in which students drop a token or ticket
- Pictorial ballot
- Write favorite on a piece of paper and drop in a ballot box

After voting day, announce the school winner and put a list of student participants in the school newsletter. Issue a press release to the local media about the school or library's participation. When notification of the state winner arrives, announce the state's winner to the students.

Nominating

Children's choice awards cannot exist without nominations of books to the award committee. Some awards allow students to nominate books while others solicit nominations from teachers, librarians, and parents. Encourage

FIGURE 2.1: Sample Press Release

FOR IMMEDIATE RELEASE

March 5, 2004

Contact: Patty Barr

Phone: 217/333-3333

White Heath Students Select Their Favorite

White Heath—Fourth grade students at White Heath Elementary School recently participated in the *Rebecca Caudill Young Readers' Book Award*. Twenty-five students were eligible to vote, and the book receiving the highest number of votes at the school was *Love That Dog* by Sharon Creech. Two students, Jay Smith and Jill Jones, read all twenty of the books on the list and received a paperback copy of one of the books from the 2005 *Rebecca Caudill Young Readers' Book Award* list. The fourth graders read a total of 203 of the nominated books since the beginning of the school year.

The *Rebecca Caudill Young Readers' Book Award* is for Illinois students in grades four through eight. Participating students must read or listen to three of the nominated books on a list of twenty fiction and non-fiction books. Those students may then vote for their favorite in February, and the votes from the state are tallied. The winning author receives the award at the Illinois School Library Media Association conference in the fall.

students to read and nominate new books for the award. Read the books yourself and ask other staff about books they have read for possible nomination. Follow the guidelines for your award's nomination process and be sure to include the nomination deadline in your time line.

Starting New Award Programs

To start a new award, find and network with other like-minded people with a love and knowledge of literature. The next steps depend on whether there is an existing award in your state.

If there is already an established award in the state but it does not cover all grade levels, the first step is to talk with the existing committee to see if they will expand their award or support the creation of a new one. The advantage of this strategy is that you draw from their experience when creating a new award. The guidelines for nomination, time line, and committee assignments for the new award can be modeled from the existing award. One key question is, "Will the new award complement or compete with the existing award?" If seeking support from an established award committee, an award that complements the existing award stands a far better chance of development. Once support is obtained, create a committee, establish guidelines, and promote the new award.

Where an award does not exist, the first step is to work with your network of like-minded people to decide the committee make up, age level of the new award, voting requirements, and criteria for selection of the books. Research the awards in other states for ideas and guidelines. Estimate the costs of running an award program. Possible expenses are postage and printing, fees for a graphic artist to design the logo, Web design and access, and bringing the winning author to the state to accept the award. Careful planning and preparation in the establishment of a new award is essential at this stage.

Once the framework and costs for the award are established, it is time to approach potential sponsors of the award. Some possible sponsors are the state library association, (especially the school or youth services division), teachers of reading associations, reading councils, and centers for the book. If at first you do not succeed, ask why the organization did not wish to help sponsor the award. With this information, revise your proposal and submit it again. The work involved in establishing and maintaining an award program is significant, but the rewards are great. Children's choice awards are a wonderful way to promote reading.

THE AWARDS

CHAPTER 3

F orty-nine states now sponsor children's choice awards, and many of these states offer multiple awards so that children of many ages have the opportunity to read and vote for their favorite picture, children's, or young adult book. The state awards in this chapter are designed to give students in grades kindergarten through twelve an opportunity to read and vote for their favorite book. Two awards, the Kansas *Heartland Award for Excellence in Young Adult Literature,* which is a national award, and the Missouri *Building Block Picture Book Award* for children of preschool age, are outside of the selected criteria for inclusion and do not appear in this chapter.

This chapter describes each award. Each entry contains the name of the state, the name on the award, and the year the first award was given. The official Web site and the relevant grade levels are on the second line. Information in five categories follows: sponsors, purpose of the award, origin of the award name (where applicable), selection criteria for books on the list, and voting requirements for the students. Where no information was available, the category does not appear in the listing. Some states do not designate a grade level, but instead use terms such as "primary, intermediate, and young adult." To be consistent, we have assigned grade levels to all awards and have listed the word designations after those grade levels.

The wording for each award's purpose was submitted by the award committees or taken directly from the Web sites and is used with permission.

The criteria for selecting the books for the lists can be quite lengthy or very short. For consistency, these terms are used:

"No books in a series" means no books such as *The Baby-Sitters Club, Fear Street,* or *Sweet Valley High.*

"No award winners" means that Newbery and Caldecott winners are not eligible for the award but the honor books are eligible.

The voting criteria often allow children to read, have read to them, or a combination of both to be eligible to vote. To indicate that this is the case for an award, we have used the words "must read or hear."

The Web sites listed as the official sites were active at the time of manuscript submission to the publisher, but please realize that Web sites have a notorious pattern of disappearing. We have arranged to mount all of the official sites listed in this book on the *Rebecca Caudill Young Readers' Book Award* Web site. You can reach this site by going to <www.rcyrba.org>.

Following the award information is a listing of all the books that have won the award, listed chronologically from the first award to the most recent. An award with several grade-level designations is arranged by year and from the youngest to the oldest (for example K-3, 4-6, 6-8, and 9-12).

For the purposes of this book, we list illustrators only for those books which are defined as "picture book," or for which kindergarten or first-grade is the lowest grade designation. Authors who illustrated their own books are not credited separately as illustrators.

ALABAMA

Emphasis on Reading—
Alabama's Children's Choice Award
1981   <www.alsde.edu>   Click on Sections,
Technology Initiatives, Library Media   K-1, 2-3, 4-6

SPONSOR: Alabama Department of Education

PURPOSE: To provide a program in which the children in the state can vote for a children's choice award.

SELECTION CRITERIA: There are three selection committees, one for each grade-level category. Books must be printed in the current year; books in series and award winners are not eligible. There are 10 books on each master list.

VOTING: There is no required number of books to read before voting, but students must read or hear the books for which they vote.

1981	K-1	*Katy No-Pocket* by Emmy Payne. H. A. Rey, ill.
	2-3	*Charlotte's Web* by E. B. White
	4-5	*The Best Christmas Pageant Ever* by Barbara Robinson
	6-8	*The Hobbit, or, There and Back Again* by J. R. R. Tolkien
	9-12	*The Acorn People* by Ron Jones
1982	K-1	*The Runaway Bunny* by Margaret Wise Brown. Clement Hurd, ill.
	2-3	*Granny and the Indians* by Peggy Parish
	4-6	*Bunnicula: A Rabbit Tale of Mystery* by James Howe
	7-9	*Mayday! Mayday!* by Hilary Milton
	10-12	*Christy* by Catherine Marshall
1983	K-1	*Sylvester and the Magic Pebble* by William Steig
	2-3	*The Chocolate Chip Mystery* by John McInnes
	4-6	*Stuart Little* by E. B. White
	7-9	*Killing Mr. Griffin* by Lois Duncan
	10-12	*Sunshine* by Norma Klein
1984	K-1	*Arthur's Nose* by Marc Brown
	2-3	*Ralph S. Mouse* by Beverly Cleary
	4-6	*Nothing's Fair in Fifth Grade* by Barthe DeClements
	7-9	*Unicorns in the Rain* by Barbara Cohen
	10-12	*Cages of Glass, Flowers of Time* by Charlotte Culin

1985	K-1	*A Pocket for Corduroy* by Don Freeman
	2-3	*The Great Green Turkey Creek Monster* by James Flora
	4-6	*The Boxcar Children* by Gertrude Chandler Warner
	7-9	*A Tangle of Roots* by Barbara Girion
	10-12	*Grendel* by John Gardner
1986	K-1	*The Pain and the Great One* by Judy Blume. Irene Trivas, ill.
	2-3	*The Adventures of Albert the Running Bear* by Barbara Isenberg. Dick Gackenbach, ill.
	4-6	*Superfudge* by Judy Blume
	7-9	*The Divorce Express* by Paula Danziger
	10-12	*Him She Loves?* by M. E. Kerr
1987	K-1	*If You Give a Mouse a Cookie* by Laura Numeroff. Felicia Bond, ill.
	2-3	*The New Kid on the Block: Poems* by Jack Prelutsky
	4-6	*Stone Fox* by John Reynolds Gardiner
	7-9	*You Never Can Tell* by Ellen Conford
	10-12	*Yeager, An Autobiography* by Chuck Yeager and Leo Janos
1988	K-1	*My Teacher Sleeps in School* by Leatie Weiss. Ellen Weiss, ill.
	2-3	*My Mother Never Listens to Me* by Marjorie Sharmat. Lynn Munsinger, ill.
	4-6	*The Dollhouse Murders* by Betty Ren Wright
	7-9	*Revenge of the Nerd* by John McNamara
	10-12	*Wart, Son of Toad* by Alden R. Carter
1989	K-1	*No Jumping on the Bed!* by Tedd Arnold
	3-5	*The War With Grandpa* by Robert Kimmel Smith
	6-8	*No Swimming in Dark Pond & Other Chilling Tales* by Judith Gorog
	9-12	*The Princess Bride: S. Morgenstern's Classic Tale of True Love and High Adventure* by William Goldman
1990	K-2	*The Little Old Man Who Could Not Read* by Irma Simonton Black. Seymour Fleishman, ill.
	3-5	*In Trouble Again, Zelda Hammersmith?* by Lynn Hall
	6-8	*Mad, Mad Monday* by Herma Silverstein
	9-12	No Award Given
1991	K-2	*The Socksnatchers* by Lorna Balian
	3-5	*More Scary Stories to Tell in the Dark* by Alvin Schwartz
	6-8	*The Glory Girl* by Betsy Byars
	9-12	*Walking Across Egypt* by Clyde Edgerton
1992	K-2	*Julius, the Baby of the World* by Kevin Henkes
	3-5	*Tales From Gold Mountain: Stories of the Chinese in the New World* by Paul Yee
	6-8	*Cousins* by Virginia Hamilton

1993	K-2	*Mucky Moose* by Jonathan Allen
	3-5	*Rats on the Roof & Other Stories* by James Marshall
	6-8	*The Day That Elvis Came to Town: A Novel* by Jan Marino
1994	K-2	*Zomo the Rabbit: A Trickster Tale from South Africa* by Gerald McDermott
	3-5	*And the Green Grass Grew All Around: Folk Poetry From Everyone* by Alvin Schwartz
	6-8	*The Pigman & Me* by Paul Zindel
1995	K-2	*Go Away, Big Green Monster!* by Ed Emberley
	3-5	*Powwow* by George Ancona
	6-8	*Anne Frank, Beyond the Diary: A Photographic Remembrance* by Ruud van der Rol
1996	K-2	*Three Star Billy* by Pat Hutchins
	3-5	*Swamp Angel* by Anne Isaacs
	6-8	*Pink and Say* by Patricia Polacco
1997	K-2	*Bamboozled* by David Legge
	3-5	*What Jamie Saw* by Carolyn Coman
	6-8	*Mick Harte Was Here* by Barbara Park
1998	K-2	*The Red Racer* by Audrey Wood
	3-5	*Strange Mysteries From Around the World* by Seymour Simon
	6-8	*Voices From the Streets: Young Former Gang Members Tell Their Stories* by S. Beth Atkin
1999	K-2	*Bunny Money* by Rosemary Wells
	3-5	*Ella Enchanted* by Gail Carson Levine
	6-8	*December* by Eve Bunting
2000	K-1	*No, David!* by David Shannon
	2-3	*Thank You, Mr. Falker* by Patricia Polacco
	4-6	*The Secret Knowledge of Grown-ups* by David Wisniewski
2001	K-2	*The Gruffalo* by Julia Donaldson. Axel Scheffler, ill.
	3-4	*Auntie Claus* by Elise Primavera
	5-6	*Lives of the Presidents: Fame, Shame (And What the Neighbors Thought)* by Kathleen Krull
2002	K-2	*Mad Dog McGraw* by Myron Uhlberg. Lydia Monks, ill.
	3-4	*Because of Winn-Dixie* by Kate DiCamillo
	5-6	*Wish You Were Here (And I Wasn't): A Book of Poems and Pictures for Globe-trotters* by Colin McNaughton
2003	K-1	*Widget* by Lyn Rossiter McFarland. Jim McFarland, ill.
	2-3	*Humpty Dumpty Egg-splodes* by Kevin O'Malley
	4-6	*A Boy at War: A Novel of Pearl Harbor* by Harry Mazer

ALASKA

See Pacific Northwest

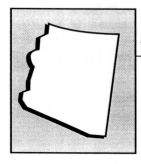

ARIZONA

Arizona Young Readers' Award
1977   <http://www.azla.org/tld/ayraindex.html>
K-3 (Picture Book), 3-6 (Intermediate Book),
6-8 (Teen Book)

SPONSOR: Arizona Library Association

PURPOSE: To stimulate the interest of young readers in outstanding literature written primarily for them. Additionally the award is to encourage
cooperation among administrators, library media specialists, and teachers in
broadening the reading programs at all levels.

SELECTION CRITERIA: To be eligible for nomination, a book must: be
a title most often read or requested by children; have strong appeal for the
age group for which the nomination is made; have been published in
English within the previous five years and still be in print.

VOTING: Qualified voters have one vote in each category for which they
qualify. To become qualified voters, young readers must read or hear at
least five of the nominated books in their category. Middle school/YA
students must read three of the 10 titles. Public library programs do not
preclude young readers participating with their class at school or in school
library programs.

1977	3-6	*Tales of a Fourth Grade Nothing* by Judy Blume
1979	3-6	*How to Eat Fried Worms* by Thomas Rockwell
1981	3-6	*Miss Nelson is Missing!* by Harry Allard and James Marshall
1983	3-6	*Superfudge* by Judy Blume
1985	3-6	*The Stupids Die* by Harry Allard
1987	3-6	*Scary Stories to Tell in the Dark* by Alvin Schwartz
1989	3-6	*The Indian in the Cupboard* by Lynne Reid Banks
1991	K-3	*The Jolly Postman, or, Other People's Letters* by Janet Ahlberg and Allan Ahlberg
	K-3	*Thomas' Snowsuit* by Robert Munsch. Michael Martchenko, ill.
	K-3	*Where's Waldo?* by Martin Handford
	3-6	*There's a Boy in the Girls' Bathroom* by Louis Sachar
	3-6	*Meanwhile, Back at the Ranch* by Trinka Hakes Noble
1993	K-3	*The Very Quiet Cricket* by Eric Carle
	3-6	*Wayside School Is Falling Down* by Louis Sachar
1994	K-3	*The Three Little Javelinas* by Susan Lowell. Jim Harris, ill.

	3-6	*Shiloh* by Phyllis Reynolds Naylor
	6-8	*Nothing But the Truth: A Documentary Novel* by Avi
1995	K-3	*The Three Little Wolves and the Big Bad Pig* by Eugene Trivizas. Helen Oxenbury, ill.
	3-6	*Totally Disgusting* by Bill Wallace
	6-8	*The Giver* by Lois Lowry
1996	K-3	*Soft Child: How Rattlesnake Got His Fangs* by Joe Hayes. Kay Sather, ill.
	3-6	*Aliens Ate My Homework* by Bruce Coville
	6-8	*Freak the Mighty* by Rodman Philbrick
1997	K-3	*The Toll-Bridge Troll* by Patricia Rae Wolff. Kimberly Bulcken Root, ill.
	3-6	*Mick Harte Was Here* by Barbara Park
	6-8	*The Name of the Game Was Murder* by Joan Lowery Nixon
1998	K-3	*Harvey Potter's Balloon Farm* by Jerdine Nolen. Mark Buehner, ill.
	3-6	*Running Out of Time* by Margaret Peterson Haddix
	6-8	*Phoenix Rising* by Karen Hesse
1999	K-3	*Stephanie's Ponytail* by Robert Munsch. Michael Martchenko, ill.
	3-6	*Drive-By* by Lynne Ewing
	6-8	*Ella Enchanted* by Gail Carson Levine
2000	K-3	*Chocolatina* by Erik Kraft. Denise Brunkus, ill.
	3-6	*Riding Freedom* by Pam Munoz Ryan
	6-8	*Harry Potter and the Sorcerer's Stone* by J. K. Rowling
2001	K-3	*What! Cried Granny: An Almost Bedtime Story* by Kate Lum. Adrian Johnson, ill.
	3-6	*Weslandia* by Paul Fleischman
	6-8	*Holes* by Louis Sachar
2002	K-3	*Bark, George* by Jules Feiffer
	3-6	*The Ghost of Fossil Glen* by Cynthia DeFelice
	6-8	*Bud, Not Buddy* by Christopher Paul Curtis
2003	K-3	*The Water Hole* by Graeme Base
	3-6	*Babe & Me: A Baseball Card Adventure* by Dan Gutman
	6-8	*Stargirl* by Jerry Spinelli

ARKANSAS

Arkansas Diamond Primary Book Award
1999   <www.asl.lib.ar.us/award.html>   K-3

SPONSOR: Arkansas Department of Education, Arkansas State Library, Arkansas Reading Association

PURPOSE: To promote thoughtful reading and discussion of books by Arkansas children in kindergarten through third grade.

NAME ORIGIN: Arkansas is known for its production of diamonds, having the only active diamond mine that is open to the public in the United States.

SELECTION CRITERIA: The reading committee begins by considering everything published in the appropriate year. Books for the 2004-2005 reading list must have been published in 2002. The author and illustrator must live in the United States. Principals, teachers, librarians, and students may nominate titles.

VOTING: Children in kindergarten through grade three must read or hear at least three of the books from the current reading list to be eligible to vote.

1999	K-3	*Roses Are Pink, Your Feet Really Stink* by Diane DeGroat
2000	K-3	*The Three Little Pigs* by Steven Kellogg
2001	K-3	*A Home for Spooky* by Gloria Rand. Ted Rand, ill.
2002	K-3	*Hooway for Wodney Wat!* by Helen Lester. Lynn Munsinger, ill.
2003	K-3	*Salt in His Shoes: Michael Jordan in Pursuit of a Dream* by Deloris Jordan and Roslyn M. Jordan. Kadir Nelson, ill.

ARKANSAS

Charlie May Simon Children's Book Award
1971   <www.asl.lib.ar.us/award.html>   4-6

SPONSOR: Arkansas Department of Education, Arkansas State Library, Arkansas Reading Association

PURPOSE: To promote better reading for children and to recognize Mrs. John Gould Fletcher, an outstanding Arkansas author who wrote under the pen name, "Charlie May Simon."

NAME ORIGIN: To honor Arkansas author Charlie May Simon. Throughout her lifetime, Mrs. Fletcher traveled extensively, gathering information for her many prize-winning biographies. During her distinguished career, Charlie May Simon wrote more than 27 books for children and young adults.

SELECTION CRITERIA: The reading committee begins by considering everything published in the appropriate year. Books for the 2004-2005 reading list must have been published in 2002. The author must be alive and must live in the United States. Principals, teachers, librarians, and students may nominate titles.

VOTING: Children in grades four through six must read or hear at least three of the books from the list to be eligible to vote.

1971	4-6	*Striped Ice Cream* by Joan Lexau
1972	4-6	*Big Ben* by David Harry Walker
1973	4-6	*Runaway Ralph* by Beverly Cleary
1974	4-6	*The Runt of Rogers School* by Harold Keith
1975	4-6	*Tales of a Fourth Grade Nothing* by Judy Blume
1976	4-6	*Bigfoot* by Hal Evarts
1977	4-6	*The Ghost on Saturday Night* by Sid Fleischman
1978	4-6	*Shoeshine Girl* by Clyde Robert Bulla
1979	4-6	*Alvin's Swap Shop* by Clifford B. Hicks
1980	4-6	*The Pinballs* by Betsy Byars
1981	4-6	*Banana Twist* by Florence Parry Heide
1982	4-6	*All the Money in the World* by Bill Brittain
1983	4-6	*Do Bananas Chew Gum?* by Jamie Gilson

1984	4-6	*Ramona Quimby, Age 8* by Beverly Cleary
1985	4-6	*Be a Perfect Person in Just Three Days* by Stephen Manes
1986	4-6	*My Horrible Secret* by Stephen Roos
1987	4-6	*The Computer Nut* by Betsy Byars
1988	4-6	*Sarah, Plain and Tall* by Patricia MacLachlan
1989	4-6	*The Whipping Boy* by Sid Fleischman
1990	4-6	*There's a Boy in the Girls' Bathroom* by Louis Sachar
1991	4-6	*All About Sam* by Lois Lowry
1992	4-6	*Number the Stars* by Lois Lowry
1993	4-6	*The Ghost Inside the Monitor* by Margaret J. Anderson
1994	4-6	*Shiloh* by Phyllis Reynolds Naylor
1995	4-6	*Attaboy, Sam!* by Lois Lowry
1996	4-6	*The Secret Funeral of Slim Jim the Snake* by Elvira Woodruff
1997	4-6	*The Best School Year Ever* by Barbara Robinson
1998	4-6	*The 13th Floor: A Ghost Story* by Sid Fleischman
1999	4-6	*Frindle* by Andrew Clements
2000	4-6	*Saving Shiloh* by Phyllis Reynolds Naylor
2001	4-6	*Flying Solo* by Ralph Fletcher
2002	4-6	*Ramona's World* by Beverly Cleary
2003	4-6	*Because of Winn-Dixie* by Kate DiCamillo

CALIFORNIA

California Young Reader Medal
1996   <www.cateweb.org>   Click CYRM and
<www.californiareads.org>   K-2 (Primary), 3-6
(Intermediate), 6-9 (Middle School/Junior High),
9-12 (Young Adult), K-12 (Picture Book for
Older Readers)

SPONSOR: California Association of Teachers of English, California Library Association, California Reading Association, California School Library Association

PURPOSE: To encourage California young readers to become better acquainted with good literature and honor favorite books and authors.

SELECTION CRITERIA: To be eligible for nomination, books must have strong appeal to the age group for which the recommendation is made; be a title most often read or requested by children and young adults; have been published within the previous five years and in print; be written by an author who is living; be an original work of fiction available in English. Young readers submit titles for nomination through their teacher or librarian.

VOTING: Students may read and vote for books in any categories, but they must read all books nominated in a category to be eligible to vote.

1996	K-2	*Stellaluna* by Janell Cannon
	3-6	*Time for Andrew: A Ghost Story* by Mary Downing Hahn
	6-9	*Freak the Mighty* by Rodman Philbrick
	9-12	*Shadow of the Dragon* by Sherry Garland
1997	K-2	*Don't Fidget a Feather!* by Erica Silverman. S. D. Schindler, ill.
	3-6	*Jennifer Murdley's Toad: A Magic Shop Book* by Bruce Coville
	6-9	*Sparrow Hawk Red* by Ben Mikaelsen
	9-12	*Staying Fat for Sarah Byrnes* by Chris Crutcher
1998	K-2	*Dog Breath!: The Horrible Trouble With Hally Tosis* by Dav Pilkey
	3-6	*The Junkyard Dog* by Erika Tamar
	6-9	*The Watson's Go to Birmingham—1963* by Christopher Paul Curtis
	9-12	*Ironman: A Novel* by Chris Crutcher

1999	K-2	*Livingstone Mouse* by Pamela Duncan Edwards. Henry Cole, ill.
	3-6	*The 13th Floor: A Ghost Story* by Sid Fleischman
	6-9	*Under the Blood-Red Sun* by Graham Salisbury
	9-12	*The Only Alien on the Planet* by Kristen D. Randle
2000	K-2	*Lost* by Paul Brett Johnson
	3-6	*Riding Freedom* by Pam Munoz Ryan
	6-9	*Ella Enchanted* by Gail Carson Levine
	9-12	*Breaking Boxes* by A. M. Jenkins
2001	K-2	*Grandpa's Teeth* by Rod Clement
	3-6	*Honus and Me: A Baseball Card Adventure* by Dan Gutman
	6-9	*Among the Hidden* by Margaret Peterson Haddix
	9-12	*Armageddon Summer* by Jane Yolen and Bruce Coville
2002	K-12	*Weslandia* by Paul Fleischman. Kevin Hawkes, ill.
	K-2	*Hooway for Wodney Wat!* by Helen Lester. Lynn Munsinger, ill.
	3-6	*The Million Dollar Shot* by Dan Gutman
	6-9	*Joey Pigza Swallowed the Key* by Jack Gantos
	9-12	*Bad* by Jean Ferris
2003	K-12	*The Babe and I* by David Adler. Terry Widener, ill.
	K-2	*I Will Never Not Ever Eat a Tomato* by Lauren Child
	3-6	*Because of Winn-Dixie* by Kate DiCamillo
	6-9	*Touching Spirit Bear* by Ben Mikaelsen
	9-12	*Define Normal* by Julie Anne Peters

COLORADO

Colorado Blue Spruce Young Adult Book Award

1985   <www.cal-webs.org/bluespruce/index.htm>   6-12

SPONSOR: Colorado Association of Libraries, Colorado Council for the International Reading Association, Colorado Language Arts Society

PURPOSE: To stimulate reading and critical thinking among teens.

NAME ORIGIN: Named after the state tree—Blue Spruce.

SELECTION CRITERIA: Nominated books: must be written by a contemporary author; must have been published within the last five years; must meet accepted standards of quality; may be fiction or nonfiction; need not have been written exclusively for a young adult audience; may not appear on the list in consecutive years; must not have appeared first as a movie or TV program; may not be written by the previous year's winning author. In addition, only one title by an author can appear on each year's list. The list contains 20 books.

VOTING: Students who have read three or more books write their choice for the year's winner in the box provided on the ballot/bookmark, and then nominate titles for next year.

1985	6-12	*Tiger Eyes* by Judy Blume
1986	6-12	*Bridge to Terabithia* by Katherine Paterson
1987	6-12	*The Third Eye* by Lois Duncan
1988	6-12	*The Other Side of Dark* by Joan Lowery Nixon
1989	6-12	*Eyes of the Dragon* by Stephen King
1990	6-12	*The Cradle Will Fall* by Mary Higgins Clark
1991	6-12	*Pet Sematary* by Stephen King
1992	6-12	*Changes in Latitude* by Will Hobbs
1993	6-12	*Jurassic Park* by Michael Crichton
1994	6-12	*It* by Stephen King
1995	6-12	*The Client* by John Grisham
1996	6-12	*The Face on the Milk Carton* by Caroline Cooney
1997	6-12	*Downriver* by Will Hobbs
1998	6-12	*Downriver* by Will Hobbs

1999	6-12	*Chicken Soup for the Teenage Soul: 101 Stories of Life, Love and Learning*
2000	6-12	*Holes* by Louis Sachar
2001	6-12	*Harry Potter and the Sorcerer's Stone* by J. K. Rowling
2002	6-12	*The Lost Boy: A Foster Child's Search for the Love of a Family* by Dave Pelzer
2003	6-12	*A Walk to Remember* by Nicholas Sparks

COLORADO

Colorado Children's Book Award
1976 <www.ccira.org/ccba.html>
K-6 (Junior Novel/Middle Grade) K-6 P
(Picture Book)

SPONSOR: The Colorado Council of the International Reading Association sponsors the award established by Dr. Bill Curtis.

PURPOSE: To encourage children's active involvement with books and reading.

SELECTION CRITERIA: Nominated books must be in print and published within the five years preceding the award year. The author of a nominated book must be living and residing in the United States. Books are not eligible if they have been nominated previously; may not be based on a movie or TV show unless the book preceded the production; may not be an award winner. Once a book in a series has won, all other books in that series by that author are not eligible. Only one title per author will be included in each year's ballot; last year's winning authors are not eligible. A book title nominated by more than one school or library is considered more heavily for inclusion in the final list.

VOTING: Each child must read or hear a minimum of three books in order to vote.

1976	K-6	*How Droofus the Dragon Lost His Head* by Bill Peet
1977	K-6	*A Day No Pigs Would Die* by Robert Newton Peck
1978	K-6	*The Sweet Touch* by Lorna Balian
1979	K-6	*The Great Green Turkey Creek Monster* by James Flora
1980	K-6	*Cloudy With a Chance of Meatballs* by Judi Barrett. Ron Barrett, ill.
1981	K-6	*Cross-Country Cat* by Mary Calhoun. Erick Ingraham, ill.
1982	K-6	*Superfudge* by Judy Blume
1983	K-6	*Space Case* by Edward Marshall. James Marshall, ill.
1984	K-6	*The Unicorn and the Lake* by Marianna Mayer. Michael Hague, ill.
1985	K-6	*Miss Nelson Is Back* by Harry Allard. James Marshall, ill.
1986	K-6	*In a Dark, Dark Room: and Other Scary Stories* by Alvin Schwartz. Dirk Zimmer, ill.

1987	K-6	*King Bidgood's in the Bathtub* by Audrey Wood. Don Wood, ill.
1988	K-6	*If You Give a Mouse a Cookie* by Laura Numeroff. Felicia Bond, ill.
1989	K-6	*The Magic School Bus at the Waterworks* by Joanna Cole. Bruce Degan, ill.
1990	K-6	*Tacky the Penguin* by Helen Lester. Lynn Munsinger, ill.
1991	K-6	*The Talking Eggs: A Folktale from the American South* by Robert D. San Souci. Jerry Pinkney, ill.
1992	K-6	*Wayside School Is Falling Down* by Louis Sachar
	K-6P	*Hershel and the Hanukkah Goblins* by Eric Kimmel. Trina Schart Hyman, ill.
1993	K-6	*Scary Stories 3: More Tales to Chill Your Bones* by Alvin Schwartz
	K-6P	*The Dog Who Had Kittens* by Polly M. Robertus. Janet Stevens, ill.
1994	K-6	*Dinotopia* by James Gurney
	K-6P	*The Stinky Cheese Man and Other Fairly Stupid Tales* by Jon Scieszka. Lane Smith, ill.
1995	K-6	*Jeremy Thatcher, Dragon Hatcher* by Bruce Coville
	K-6P	*Coyote Steals the Blanket: A Ute Tale* by Janet Stevens
1996	K-6	*The Best School Year Ever* by Barbara Robinson
	K-6P	*Arthur's Chicken Pox* by Marc Brown
1997	K-6	*Wayside School Gets a Little Stranger* by Louis Sachar
	K-6P	*Piggie Pie* by Margie Palatini. Howard Fine, ill.
1998	K-6	*Shiloh Season* by Phyllis Reynolds Naylor
	K-6P	*Ten Little Dinosaurs* by Pattie L. Schnetzler. Jim Harris, ill.
1999	K-6	*The Adventures of Captain Underpants: An Epic Novel* by Dav Pilkey
	K-6P	*Parts* by Tedd Arnold
2000	K-6	*Saving Shiloh* by Phyllis Reynolds Naylor
	K-6P	*Psssst! It's Me...The Bogeyman!* by Barbara Park. Stephen Kroninger, ill.
2001	K-6	*Bunnicula Strikes Again* by James Howe
	K-6P	*Hooway for Wodney Wat!* by Helen Lester. Lynn Munsinger, ill.
2002	K-6	*Ghosts of the White House* by Cheryl Harness
	K-6P	*David Goes to School* by David Shannon
2003	K-6	*The Bad Beginning* by Lemony Snicket
	K-6P	*Baloney, Henry P.* by Jon Scieszka. Lane Smith, ill.

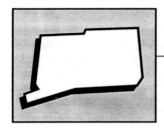

CONNECTICUT

Nutmeg Children's Book Award
1993   <www.biblio.org/nutmegaward>   4-6

SPONSOR: Connecticut Library Association, Connecticut Educational Media Association

PURPOSE: To encourage children in Connecticut to read fiction for enjoyment, promote teacher and library involvement in children's literature programs, commend authors of children's fiction, promote the use of libraries and media centers, and increase community support and involvement in developing children's interest in reading.

NAME ORIGIN: Named after the state nickname—Nutmeg State.

SELECTION CRITERIA: Nominated books must be copyrighted in the United States within the last five years preceding the nomination year and written by an author residing in the United States; all authors will be considered, especially those of the Northeast region. The books must be in print in paperback, have a well-constructed plot and defined story structure, strong characterization, striking language, vivid setting, and appeal for readers in grades four through six.

VOTING: Children in grades four through six can vote for the winning title in either their school library media center or at their public library.

1993	4-6	*My Teacher Is an Alien* by Bruce Coville
1994	4-6	*Shiloh* by Phyllis Reynolds Naylor
1995	4-6	*The Biggest Klutz in Fifth Grade* by Bill Wallace
1996	4-6	*The Grand Escape* by Phyllis Reynolds Naylor
1997	4-6	*Shape-Changer* by Bill Brittain
1998	4-6	*The Private Notebook of Katie Roberts, Age 11* by Amy Hest
1999	4-6	*Mick Harte Was Here* by Barbara Park
2000	4-6	*The Million Dollar Shot* by Dan Gutman
2001	4-6	*101 Ways to Bug Your Parents* by Lee Wardlaw
2002	4-6	*Among the Hidden* by Margaret Peterson Haddix
2003	4-6	*Because of Winn-Dixie* by Kate DiCamillo
2004	4-6	*Babe & Me: A Baseball Card Adventure* by Dan Gutman

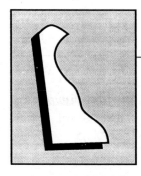

DELAWARE

Blue Hen Book Award
1996   K-8 P (Picture Books), K-8 C (Chapter Books)

SPONSOR: Children's Services Division of the Delaware Library Association

NAME ORIGIN: Named after the state bird—Blue Hen Chicken.

VOTING: Only children age 14 and under may vote. They must read at least five of the nominated books and may vote only once.

1996	K-3	*Harvey Potter's Balloon Farm* by Jerdine Nolen. Mark Buehner, ill.
1997	K-3	*Miss Bindergarten Gets Ready for Kindergarten* by Joseph Slate. Ashley Wolff, ill.
1998	K-3	No Award Given
1999	K-3	*Grandpa's Teeth* by Rod Clement
2000	K-3	*A Bad Case of Stripes* by David Shannon
2001	K-8 C	*Harry Potter and the Sorcerer's Stone* by J. K. Rowling
	K-8 P	*Hooway for Wodney Wat!* by Helen Lester. Lynn Munsinger, ill.
2002	K-8 C	*Because of Winn-Dixie* by Kate DiCamillo
	K-8 P	*Dogs' Night* by Meredith Hooper. Allan Curless and Mark Burgess, ill.
2003	K-8 C	*Artemis Fowl* by Eoin Colfer
	K-8 P	*The Great Gracie Chase* by Cynthia Rylant. Mark Teague, ill.

DELAWARE

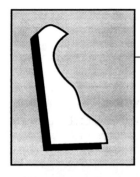

Delaware Diamonds Primary Award
1991   <www.doe.state.de.us/dsra/
Delaware_Diamonds.html>   K-2, 3-5

SPONSOR: Diamond State Reading Association

PURPOSE: To encourage young readers in Delaware to become better acquainted with quality literature, to honor favorite books and authors, and to broaden students' awareness of literature as a lifelong pleasure.

NAME ORIGIN: Named after the state nickname—Diamond State.

VOTING: In order to be eligible to vote, kindergarten through second grade students must read or hear eight of the 10 nominated books. Third through fifth grade students must read or hear five of the eight nominated books.

1991	K-2	*Cloudy With a Chance of Meatballs* by Judi Barrett. Ron Barrett, ill.
	3-5	*Nothing's Fair in Fifth Grade* by Barthe DeClements
1992		No Award Given
1993	K-2	*Sam's Sandwich* by David Pelham
	3-5	*There's a Boy in the Girls' Bathroom* by Louis Sachar
1994	K-2	*The Talking Eggs: A Folktale from the American South* by Robert D. San Souci. Jerry Pinkney, ill.
	3-5	*Maniac Magee* by Jerry Spinelli
1995	K-2	*Tom* by Tomie dePaola
	3-5	*Shiloh* by Phyllis Reynolds Naylor
1996	K-2	*Stellaluna* by Janell Cannon
	3-5	*The Mouse and the Motorcycle* by Beverly Cleary
1997	K-2	*Thomas' Snowsuit* by Robert Munsch. Michael Martchenko, ill.
	3-5	*If You're Not Here, Please Raise Your Hand: Poems About School* by Kalli Dakos
1998	K-2	*Dinosaurs Before Dark* by Mary Pope Osborne. Sal Murdocca, ill.
	3-5	*Junebug* by Alice Mead
1999	K-2	*Sam and the Tigers: A New Telling of Little Black Sambo* by Julius Lester. Jerry Pinkney, ill.

	3-5	*Frindle* by Andrew Clements
2000	K-2	*Alligator Baby* by Robert Munsch. Michael Martchenko, ill.
	(3-5)	*Hey, New Kid!* by Betsy Duffey
2001	K-2	*Junie B. Jones Is Not a Crook* by Barbara Park
	(3-5)	*Summer Reading Is Killing Me!* by Jon Scieszka
2002	K-2	*Hooway for Wodney Wat!* by Helen Lester. Lynn Munsinger, ill.
	3-5	*Dear Mrs. Ryan, You're Ruining My Life* by Jennifer B. Jones
2003	K-2	*Jingle Bells, Homework Smells* by Diane DeGroat
	3-5	*Lenny and Mel* by Erik P. Kraft

FLORIDA

Florida Children's Book Award
1989   <www.flreads.org/>   Click on
Children's Book Award   K-2

SPONSOR: Florida Reading Association

PURPOSE: To encourage young children to become enthusiastic about books.

SELECTION CRITERIA: The books selected must have been copyrighted within the last five years and in print.

VOTING: Children must read at least five of the eight books to be eligible to vote.

1989	K-2	*The Jolly Postman, or, Other People's Letters* by Janet Ahlberg and Allan Ahlberg
1990	K-2	*There's an Alligator Under My Bed* by Mercer Mayer
1991	K-2	*The Magic School Bus at the Waterworks* by Joanna Cole. Bruce Degan, ill.
1992	K-2	*Weird Parents* by Audrey Wood
1993	K-2	*Rhinos for Lunch and Elephants for Supper! A Maasai Tale* by Tololwa M. Mollel. Barbara Spurll, ill.
1994	K-2	*Zomo the Rabbit: A Trickster Tale from South Africa* by Gerald McDermott
1995	K-2	*The Rainbow Fish* by Marcus Pfister
1996	K-2	*Can I Have a Stegosaurus, Mom? Can I? Please!?* by Lois Grambling. H. B. Lewis, ill.
1997	K-2	*Officer Buckle and Gloria* by Peggy Rathman
1998	K-2	*The Toll-Bridge Troll* by Patricia Rae Wolff. Kimberly Bulcken Root, ill.
1999	K-2	*Parts* by Tedd Arnold
2000	K-2	*Mouse, Look Out!* by Judy Waite. Norma Burgin, ill.
2001	K-2	*Mr. Tanen's Ties* by Maryann Cocca-Leffler
2002	K-2	*Bark, George* by Jules Feiffer
2003	K-2	*A Spoon for Every Bite* by Joe Hayes. Rebecca Leer, ill.

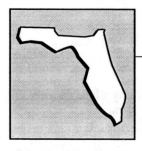

FLORIDA

Sunshine State Young Reader's Award
1984   <www.firn.edu/doe/bin00015/ssyrap.htm>
3-5, 6-8

SPONSOR: School Library Media Services, Office of the Department of Education, Florida Association for Media in Education

PURPOSE: To encourage students to read for personal satisfaction; to help students in understanding, relating to, and enjoying life through experiences with literature; to help students become discriminating readers in their personal selection of books; to develop an awareness of outstanding literature for children and young people; to encourage cooperation among administrators, library media specialists, and teachers in broadening reading experiences; to give recognition to those who write books for children and young people.

NAME ORIGIN: Named after the state nickname—Sunshine State.

SELECTION CRITERIA: Florida media specialists nominate all books considered for the list. The qualifications for the books are: must be works of fiction; the author must be living and reside in or be a citizen of the United States; and the book's copyright should be within the past four years. If a book does not make the list at a selection meeting for one year, it remains on the nominations list until it is not eligible by date.

VOTING: Students must read three books from the list to be eligible to vote.

1984	3-8	*Bunnicula: A Rabbit Tale of Mystery* by James Howe
1985	3-8	*Superfudge* by Judy Blume
1986	3-8	*Be a Perfect Person in Just Three Days!* by Stephen Manes
1987	3-8	*Thirteen Ways to Sink a Sub* by Jamie Gilson
1988	3-8	*Sixth Grade Can Really Kill You* by Barthe DeClements
1989	3-8	*The Sixth Grade Sleepover* by Eve Bunting
1990	3-5	*Teacher's Pet* by Johanna Horwitz
	6-8	*Trapped in Death Cave* by Bill Wallace
1991	3-5	*There's a Boy in the Girls' Bathroom* by Louis Sachar
	6-8	*There's a Boy in the Girls' Bathroom* by Louis Sachar
1992	3-5	*Fudge* by Charlotte Graeber

	6-8	*Something Upstairs: A Tale of Ghosts* by Avi
1993	3-5	*Fudge-A-Mania* by Judy Blume
	6-8	*Nightmare* by Willo Davis Roberts
1994	3-5	*The Summer I Shrank My Grandmother* by Elvira Woodruff
	6-8	*The True Confessions of Charlotte Doyle* by Avi
1995	3-5	*Knights of the Kitchen Table* by Jon Scieszka
	6-8	*Devil's Bridge* by Cynthia DeFelice
1996	3-5	*Blackwater Swamp* by Bill Wallace
	6-8	*Seventh Grade Weirdo* by Lee Wardlaw
1997	3-5	*Nasty, Stinky Sneakers* by Eve Bunting
	6-8	*Nasty, Stinky Sneakers* by Eve Bunting
1998	3-5	*Tornado* by Betsy Byars
	6-8	*Ghosts Don't Get Goose Bumps* by Elvira Woodruff
1999	3-5	*101 Ways to Bug Your Parents* by Lee Wardlaw
	6-8	*101 Ways to Bug Your Parents* by Lee Wardlaw
2000	3-5	*The Volcano Disaster* by Peg Kehret
	6-8	*Jaguar* by Roland Smith
2001	3-5	*The Ghost in Room 11* by Betty Ren Wright
	6-8	*The Ghost of Fossil Glen* by Cynthia DeFelice
2002	3-5	*Because of Winn-Dixie* by Kate DiCamillo
	6-8	*Among the Hidden* by Margaret Peterson Haddix
2003	3-5	*Holes* by Louis Sachar
	6-8	*Holes* by Louis Sachar

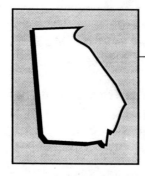

GEORGIA

Georgia Children's Literature Book Award
1969   <www.coe.uga.edu/gachildlit/awards/
index.html>   K-4 (Picture Storybook), 4-8
(Children's Book)

SPONSOR: Department of Language Education, College of Education, University of Georgia

SELECTION CRITERIA: Only fiction titles published within the past five years and in print are eligible. Award winners are ineligible. Only one title by an author may be included on the list; an illustrator or author may appear more than once on the Picture Storybook list if teamed with another person; nominated authors and illustrators must be alive and living in North America. Authors and illustrators with books on preceding lists may be repeated, but not their books; winning authors and illustrators will be excluded from the competition the following year. Books nominated for the awards should have literary and artistic merit and be free of negative stereotyping. The list includes 20 titles.

VOTING: Students in kindergarten through fourth grade must read or hear 10 books to be eligible to vote; students in grades four through eight must read or hear three books to be eligible to vote. Fourth grade students may vote on either list but not both.

1969	4-8	*Skinny* by Robert Burch
1970	4-8	*Ramona the Pest* by Beverly Cleary
1971	4-8	*Queenie Peavy* by Robert Burch
1972	4-8	*J. T.* by Jane Wagner
1973	4-8	*Hey, What's Wrong With This One?* by Maia Wojciechowska
1974	4-8	*Doodle and the Go-Cart* by Robert Burch
1975	4-8	*A Taste of Blackberries* by Doris Buchanan Smith
1976	4-8	*The Best Christmas Pageant Ever* by Barbara Robinson
1977	K-4	*Alexander and the Terrible, Horrible, No Good, Very Bad Day* by Judith Viorst. Ray Cruz, ill.
	4-8	*Tales of a Fourth Grade Nothing* by Judy Blume
1978	K-4	*The Sweet Touch* by Lorna Balian
	4-8	*Freaky Friday* by Mary Rodgers
1979	K-4	*Big Bad Bruce* by Bill Peet
	4-8	*The Pinballs* by Betsy Byars

1980	K-4	*Miss Nelson is Missing!* by Harry Allard and James Marshall
	4-8	*The Great Brain Does It Again* by John D. Fitzgerald
1981	K-4	*Tailypo!* by Jan Wahl. Wil Clay, ill.
	4-8	*The Great Gilly Hopkins* by Katherine Paterson
1982	K-4	*Pinkerton, Behave!* by Steven Kellogg
	4-8	*Don't Hurt Laurie!* by Willo Davis Roberts
1983	K-4	*Herbie's Troubles* by Carol Chapman. Kelly Oechsli, ill.
	4-8	*Superfudge* by Judy Blume
1984	K-4	*Cloudy With a Chance of Meatballs* by Judi Barrett. Ron Barrett, ill.
	4-8	*Nothing's Fair in Fifth Grade* by Barthe DeClements
1985	K-4	*Doctor DeSoto* by William Steig
	4-8	*Skinnybones* by Barbara Park
1986	K-4	*The Unicorn and the Lake* by Marianna Mayer. Michael Hague, ill.
	4-8	*The Secret Life of the Underwear Champ* by Betty Miles
1987	K-4	*My Teacher Sleeps in School* by Leatie Weiss. Ellen Weiss, ill.
	4-8	*Be a Perfect Person in Just Three Days!* by Stephen Manes
1988	K-4	*If You Give a Mouse a Cookie* by Laura Numeroff. Felicia Bond, ill.
	4-8	*Christina's Ghost* by Betty Ren Wright
1989	K-4	*Max, the Bad Talking Parrot* by Patricia Brennan Demuth. Bo Zaunders, ill.
	4-8	*The War With Grandpa* by Robert Kimmel Smith
1990	K-4	*No Jumping on the Bed!* by Tedd Arnold
	4-8	*There's a Boy in the Girls' Bathroom* by Louis Sachar
1991	K-4	*We're Back! A Dinosaur's Story* by Hudson Talbott
	4-8	*Hatchet* by Gary Paulsen
1992	K-4	*Two Bad Ants* by Chris Van Allsburg
	4-8	*All About Sam* by Lois Lowry
1993	K-4	*The Talking Eggs: A Folktale from the American South* by Robert D. San Souci. Jerry Pinkney, ill.
	4-8	*The Doll in the Garden: A Ghost Story* by Mary Downing Hahn
1994	K-4	*The Rough-Face Girl* by Rafe Martin. David Shannon, ill.
	4-8	*Jennifer Murdley's Toad: A Magic Shop Book* by Bruce Coville
1995	K-4	*Hurricane City* by Sarah Weeks. James Warhola, ill.
	4-8	*Mayfield Crossing* by Vaunda M. Nelson
1996	K-4	*Martha Speaks* by Susan Meddaugh
	4-8	*Time for Andrew: A Ghost Story* by Mary Downing Hahn
1997	K-4	*The Stinky Cheese Man and Other Fairly Stupid Tales* by Jon Scieszka. Lane Smith, ill.
	4-8	*Mick Harte Was Here* by Barbara Park

1998	K-4	*Dog Breath!: The Horrible Trouble With Hally Tosis* by Dav Pilkey
	4-8	*The Best School Year Ever* by Barbara Robinson
1999	K-4	*Leo the Magnificat* by Ann M. Martin. Emily Arnold McCully, ill.
	4-8	*Frindle* by Andrew Clements
2000	K-4	*No, David!* by David Shannon
	4-8	*The Imp That Ate My Homework* by Laurence Yep
2001	K-4	*Verdi* by Janell Cannon
	4-8	*My Life as a Fifth-Grade Comedian* by Elizabeth Levy
2002	K-4	*Bark, George* by Jules Feiffer
	4-8	*Danger in the Desert* by Terri Fields
2003	K-4	*Stand Tall, Molly Lou Melon* by Patty Lovell. David Catrow, ill.
	4-8	*The Power of Un* by Nancy Etchemendy

HAWAII

The Nene Award
1964 <http://nene.k12.hi.us> 4-6

SPONSOR: Hawaii Library Association's Children and Youth Section, the Hawaii Association of School Librarians, Hawaii State Public Library System, Hawaii Department of Education

PURPOSE: To encourage all the children of Hawaii to "thrill" to the "best" of the new books published.

NAME ORIGIN: Named after the state bird—Nene.

SELECTION CRITERIA: Every child in Hawaii in grades four through six is encouraged to select a book suitable for the Nene Award. Selection now consists of 20 of the top "vote getters," and 20 titles from public and school librarians. Approximately 35-40 titles comprise the suggested reading list.

VOTING: Students vote for one book. No required number of books must be read to be eligible to vote.

1964	4-6	*Island of the Blue Dolphins* by Scott O'Dell
1965	4-6	*Mary Poppins* by P. L. Travers
1966	4-6	*Old Yeller* by Fred Gipson
1967	4-6	No Award Given
1968	4-6	*Ribsy* by Beverly Cleary
1969	4-6	*The Mouse and the Motorcycle* by Beverly Cleary
1970	4-6	*Henry Reed's Baby-sitting Service* by Keith Robertson
1971	4-6	*Ramona the Pest* by Beverly Cleary
1972	4-6	*Runaway Ralph* by Beverly Cleary
1973	4-6	*Sounder* by William Armstrong
1974	4-6	*Jonathan Livingston Seagull* by Richard Bach
1975	4-6	*Are You There, God? It's Me, Margaret* by Judy Blume
1976	4-6	*How to Eat Fried Worms* by Thomas Rockwell
1977	4-6	*Freaky Friday* by Mary Rodgers
1978	4-6	*Charlie and the Great Glass Elevator* by Roald Dahl
1979	4-6	*Ramona and Her Father* by Beverly Cleary
1980	4-6	*The Cat Ate My Gymsuit* by Paula Danziger
1981	4-6	*My Robot Buddy* by Alfred Slote

1982	4-6	*Superfudge* by Judy Blume
1983	4-6	*Bunnicula: A Rabbit Tale of Mystery* by James Howe
1984	4-6	*Nothing's Fair in Fifth Grade* by Barthe DeClements
1985	4-6	*Jelly Belly* by Robert Kimmel Smith
1986	4-6	*Be a Perfect Person in Just Three Days!* by Stephen Manes
1987	4-6	*Karen Kepplewhite is the World's Best Kisser* by Eve Bunting
1988	4-6	*You Shouldn't Have to Say Good-Bye* by Patricia Hermes
1989	4-6	*Dear Mr. Henshaw* by Beverly Cleary
1990	4-6	*Fudge* by Charlotte Graeber
1991	4-6	*There's a Boy in the Girls' Bathroom* by Louis Sachar
1992	4-6	*The Whipping Boy* by Sid Fleischman
1993	4-6	*Fudge-A-Mania* by Judy Blume
1994	4-6	*Shiloh* by Phyllis Reynolds Naylor
1995	4-6	*My Teacher Is an Alien* by Bruce Coville
1996	4-6	*Maniac Magee* by Jerry Spinelli
1997	4-6	*Ghosts in Fourth Grade* by Constance Hiser
1998	4-6	*Under the Blood-Red Sun* by Graham Salisbury
1999	4-6	*The Best School Year Ever* by Barbara Robinson
2000	4-6	*Harry Potter and the Sorcerer's Stone* by J. K. Rowling
2001	4-6	*Holes* by Louis Sachar
2002	4-6	*Bud, Not Buddy* by Christopher Paul Curtis
2003	4-6	*The Bad Beginning* by Lemony Snicket

IDAHO

See Pacific Northwest

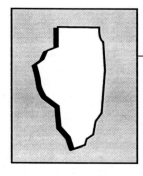

ILLINOIS

Abraham Lincoln Illinois High School Book Award
2005   <www.islma.org>   9-12

SPONSOR: Illinois School Library Media Association

PURPOSE: To encourage high school students to read for personal satisfaction and become familiar with young adult authors.

NAME ORIGIN: Abraham Lincoln was one of Illinois' best known residents and an avid reader.

SELECTION CRITERIA: Books nominated may be fiction, nonfiction, or poetry; author living at the time of list selection; should be available in paperback; may not be a textbook, a translation, or an anthology by more than one author; and should have a copyright date within the last 10 years. There are 22 books on the list.

VOTING: Students must read or listen to at least five books to be eligible to vote.

ILLINOIS

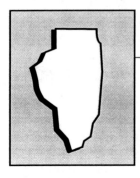

Monarch Award

2005   <http://www.islma.org/grants_awards.htm#monarch>   K-3

SPONSOR: Illinois School Library Media Association

PURPOSE: To encourage Illinois students to read critically and to become familiar with children's books, authors, and illustrators.

NAME ORIGIN: Named after the state insect—the Monarch butterfly. The butterfly symbolizes growth, change, and freedom—qualities that also characterize the emergent reader.

SELECTION CRITERIA: To be eligible for the list, books must meet the following criteria: published within the past five years; currently in print; author and illustrator living at time of the list selection; and fiction or nonfiction in the following genre: picture books, early reading books, or early chapter books.

VOTING: To be eligible to vote, children must read or hear at least five books on the list.

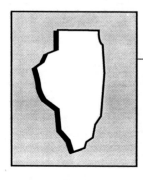

ILLINOIS

Rebecca Caudill Young Readers' Book Award
1988   <www.rcyrba.org>   4-8

SPONSOR: Illinois Reading Council, Illinois Association of Teachers of English, Illinois School Library Media Association. Administered by the *Rebecca Caudill Young Readers' Book Award* Steering Committee

PURPOSE: To encourage children and young adults to read for personal satisfaction; to develop a statewide awareness of outstanding literature for children and young people and to promote a desire for literacy; to encourage cooperation among Illinois agencies providing educational and library service to young people.

NAME ORIGIN: The award is named in honor of Rebecca Caudill, who lived and wrote in Urbana, Illinois for nearly 50 years.

SELECTION CRITERIA: Students, teachers, library media specialists, and public librarians may nominate books. All nominations must be received on the official form to be considered. The criteria for nomination are: the nominator must have read the book; books must have literary merit; be of interest and appeal to children in grades four through eight; must be copyrighted within the last five years; be in print at the time of selection; may be nonfiction, poetry, or fiction, but may not be a textbook, an anthology, a translation, part of a series or formula fiction. The author must be living at the time of nomination and at the time of selection to the list.

VOTING: Each student must read or hear three books in order to be eligible to vote.

1988	4-8	*The Indian in the Cupboard* by Lynne Reid Banks
1989	4-8	*The Dollhouse Murders* by Betty Ren Wright
1990	4-8	*Wait Till Helen Comes* by Mary Downing Hahn
1991	4-8	*Matilda* by Roald Dahl
1992	4-8	*Number the Stars* by Lois Lowry
1993	4-8	*Maniac Magee* by Jerry Spinelli
1994	4-8	*Shiloh* by Phyllis Reynolds Naylor
1995	4-8	*Flight #116 Is Down* by Caroline Cooney

1996	4-8	*The Giver* by Lois Lowry
1997	4-8	*The Best School Year Ever* by Barbara Robinson
1998	4-8	*Mick Harte Was Here* by Barbara Park
1999	4-8	*Frindle* by Andrew Clements
2000	4-8	*Ella Enchanted* by Gail Carson Levine
2001	4-8	*Harry Potter and the Sorcerer's Stone* by J. K. Rowling
2002	4-8	*Holes* by Louis Sachar
2003	(4-8)	*Fever, 1793* by Laurie Halse Anderson

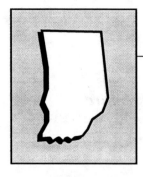

INDIANA

Eliot Rosewater Indiana High School Book Award
1996   <http://www.ilfonline.org/Units/Associations/
aime/Programs/Rosie/rosie.htm>   9-12

SPONSOR: Association for Indiana Media Educators, administered by the *Eliot Rosewater Indiana High School Book Award* Committee (Rosie Committee)

PURPOSE: To encourage high school students to read for fun and promote cooperation between school administrators, library media specialists, teachers, and public librarians in broadening reading programs. The *Rosie Award* promotes reading across the curriculum.

NAME ORIGIN: Eliot Rosewater is a recurring fictional character in Kurt Vonnegut's novels, including *God Bless You, Mr. Rosewater*. Vonnegut is a famous Hoosier author who grew up in Indianapolis. This award was named to honor him and all Indiana writers. The award is often referred to as the "Rosie Award" or "Rosie."

SELECTION CRITERIA: A book is eligible for nomination if it is in print at the time of nomination and has not been a previous nominee.

VOTING: Students must read five books to be eligible to vote.

1996	9-12	*They Cage the Animals at Night* by Jennings Michael Burch
1997	9-12	*The Giver* by Lois Lowry
1998	9-12	*It Happened to Nancy* by Anonymous Teenager
1999	9-12	*Driver's Ed* by Caroline Cooney
2000	9-12	*Where the Heart Is* by Billie Letts
2001	9-12	*Harry Potter and the Sorcerer's Stone* by J. K. Rowling
2002	9-12	*Imani All Mine* by Connie Porter
2003	9-12	*Dreamland: A Novel* by Sarah Dessen

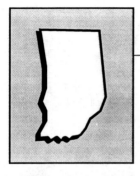

INDIANA

Young Hoosier Book Award
1975 <www.ilfonline.org/Programs/YHBA/yhba.htm> K-3, 4-6, 6-8

SPONSOR: Association for Indiana Media Educators, Indiana Library Federation

PURPOSE: To stimulate recreational reading among elementary and middle school/junior high school children and to encourage cooperation between administrators, library media specialists, teachers, public libraries, and the community in providing reading experiences for Indiana school children.
NAME ORIGIN: Named after the state nickname—Hoosier State.

SELECTION CRITERIA: The author or illustrator of a nominated book will be restricted to one work in any particular year; must be living and residing in the United States. Books must have been published within the last five years; be in print at the time of selection; cannot be a previous nominee or award winner.

VOTING: Each student who has read or heard at least 12 of the kindergarten through third grade nominees or five of the nominated books in the other categories is eligible to vote.

1975	4-6	*The Trumpet of the Swan* by E. B. White
1976	4-6	*Are You There, God? It's Me, Margaret* by Judy Blume
1977	4-6	*How to Eat Fried Worms* by Thomas Rockwell
1978	4-6	*The Best Christmas Pageant Ever* by Barbara Robinson
1979	4-6	*The Ghost on Saturday Night* by Sid Fleischman
1980	4-6	*Don't Hurt Laurie!* by Willo Davis Roberts
1981	4-6	*The Goof That Won the Pennant* by Jonah Kalb
1982	4-6	*Help! I'm a Prisoner in the Library* by Eth Clifford
1983	4-6	*Superfudge* by Judy Blume
1984	4-6	*Jelly Belly* by Robert Kimmel Smith
1985	4-6	*Operation Dump the Chump* by Barbara Park
1986	4-6	*When the Boys Ran the House* by Joan Carris
	6-8	*Stranger With My Face* by Lois Duncan
1987	4-6	*Baby-Sitting is a Dangerous Job* by Willo Davis Roberts

	6-8	*A Deadly Game of Magic* by Joan Lowery Nixon
1988	4-6	*The War With Grandpa* by Robert Kimmel Smith
	6-8	No Award Given
1989	4-6	*Christina's Ghost* by Betty Ren Wright
	6-8	*Wait Till Helen Comes* by Mary Downing Hahn
1990	4-6	*Fudge* by Charlotte Graeber
	6-8	*The Dark and Deadly Pool* by Joan Lowery Nixon
1991	4-6	*Ten Kids, No Pets* by Ann M. Martin
	6-8	*Hatchet* by Gary Paulsen
1992	K-3	*Heckedy Peg* by Audrey Wood. Don Wood, ill.
	4-6	*Nightmare Mountain* by Peg Kehret
	6-8	*Don't Look Behind You* by Lois Duncan
1993	K-3	*Tuesday* by David Wiesner
	4-6	*The Dead Man in Indian Creek* by Mary Downing Hahn
	6-8	*The Face on the Milk Carton* by Caroline Cooney
1994	K-3	*The Dog Who Had Kittens* by Polly M. Robertus. Janet Stevens, ill.
	4-6	*Shiloh* by Phyllis Reynolds Naylor
	6-8	*Strider* by Beverly Cleary
1995	K-3	*The Enchanted Wood: An Original Fairy Tale* by Ruth Sanderson
	4-6	*Horror at the Haunted House* by Peg Kehret
	6-8	*Whispers From the Dead* by Joan Lowery Nixon
1996	K-3	*Zomo the Rabbit: A Trickster Tale from South Africa* by Gerald McDermott
	4-6	*A Ghost in the House* by Betty Ren Wright
	6-8	*Nightjohn* by Gary Paulsen
1997	K-3	*Harvey Potter's Balloon Farm* by Jerdine Nolen. Mark Buehner, ill.
	4-6	*Wayside School Gets a Little Stranger* by Louis Sachar
	6-8	No Award Given
1998	K-3	*Heart of a Tiger* by Marsha Diane Arnold. Jamichael Henterly, ill.
	4-6	*Mick Harte Was Here* by Barbara Park
	6-8	*The Doom Stone* by Paul Zindel
1999	K-3	*My Little Sister Ate One Hare* by Bill Grossman. Kevin Hawkes, ill.
	4-6	*Frindle* by Andrew Clements
	6-8	*Twisted Summer* by Willo Davis Roberts
2000	K-3	*Double Trouble in Walla Walla* by Andrew Clements. Sal Murdocca, ill.
	4-6	*Saving Shiloh* by Phyllis Reynolds Naylor

	6-8	*Ella Enchanted* by Gail Carson Levine
2001	K-3	*Akiak: A Tale from the Iditarod* by Robert J. Blake
	4-6	*Small Steps: The Year I Got Polio* by Peg Kehret
	6-8	*Forged By Fire* by Sharon Draper
2002	K-3	*Hooway for Wodney Wat!* by Helen Lester. Lynn Munsinger, ill.
	4-6	*Cliff Hanger* by Gloria Skurzynski
	6-8	*Among the Hidden* by Margaret Peterson Haddix
2003	K-3	*Mr. Tanen's Ties* by Maryann Cocca-Leffler
	4-6	*Because of Winn-Dixie* by Kate DiCamillo
	6-8	*Stargirl* by Jerry Spinelli

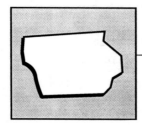

IOWA

Iowa Children's Choice Award
1980   <www.iema-ia.org/icca.html>   3-6

SPONSOR: Iowa Educational Media Association

PURPOSE: To encourage children to read more and better books; to discriminate in choosing worthwhile books; to provide an avenue for positive dialogue between teachers, parents, and children about books and authors; to give recognition to those who write books for children.

SELECTION CRITERIA: The author must be alive and residing in the United States and only one title per author is allowed on the list. Books must be an original work of fiction in English; been published in hardcover; be in print; and published within the four years previous to the year of nomination. Nonfiction is acceptable if there is a definite story line, and picture books, if included, must be illustrated by the author. Books that have appeared on any previous ICCA master list are excluded, as are award winners; books that are a retelling of fables, folklore, newly illustrated songs or nursery rhymes and adaptations (TV, movies, etc.). Books on the list must have a reading/interest level for grades three through six; be appropriate in content, of high literary quality, and appealing to children; well balanced with a wide range of interests and reading levels represented. The number of books on the master list will be flexible with a minimum of 15 and a maximum of 25 for any one year.

VOTING: Students must read or hear at least two titles to be eligible to vote. Students vote for only one title and may not vote for any title they have not read or heard.

1980	3-6	*How to Eat Fried Worms* by Thomas Rockwell
1981	3-6	*The Great Gilly Hopkins* by Katherine Paterson
1982	3-6	*Bunnicula: A Rabbit Tale of Mystery* by James Howe
1983	3-6	*Superfudge* by Judy Blume
1984	3-6	*Nothing's Fair in Fifth Grade* by Barthe DeClements
1985	3-6	*Ralph S. Mouse* by Beverly Cleary
1986	3-6	*When the Boys Ran the House* by Joan Carris
1987	3-6	*Ramona Forever* by Beverly Cleary
1988	3-6	*The Dollhouse Murders* by Betty Ren Wright
1989	3-6	*Night of the Twisters* by Ivy Ruckman

1990	3-6	*Wait Till Helen Comes* by Mary Downing Hahn
1991	3-6	*There's a Boy in the Girls' Bathroom* by Louis Sachar
1992	3-6	*Fudge* by Charlotte Graeber
1993	3-6	*Fudge-A-Mania* by Judy Blume
1994	3-6	*Nightmare Mountain* by Peg Kehret
1995	3-6	*Attaboy, Sam!* by Lois Lowry
1996	3-6	*Terror at the Zoo* by Peg Kehret
1997	3-6	*The Best School Year Ever* by Barbara Robinson
1998	3-6	*Mick Harte Was Here* by Barbara Park
1999	3-6	*Shiloh Season* by Phyllis Reynolds Naylor
2000	3-6	*Saving Shiloh* by Phyllis Reynolds Naylor
2001	3-6	*The Million Dollar Shot* by Dan Gutman
2002	3-6	*The Ghost of Fossil Glen* by Cynthia DeFelice
2003	3-6	*Because of Winn-Dixie* by Kate DiCamillo

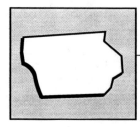

IOWA

Iowa High School Book Award

2004   <www.iema-ia.org/ihsbaindex.html>   9-12

SPONSOR: Iowa Educational Media Association

PURPOSE: To provide a high quality, varied reading list for grades nine through twelve that allows for input from the teenage reader and encourages pleasure reading.

SELECTION CRITERIA: Students make nominations. The nominated titles must be published within the previous three years at the time of nomination (books nominated in 2004 will have a copyright date of 2001 or newer). One selection on the list is allowed per author. Selected titles must have a favorable review in at least one major reviewing periodical. Books in a series will be allowed (for example, *Daughter of the Forest* by Marrilier), but books that are novelizations of movies or TV programs are not included (such as *Dead Poets Society* by Kleinbaum). When feasible, Iowa authors are included on the list.

VOTING: Students must read two books from the list to be eligible to vote.

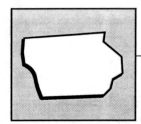

IOWA

Iowa Teen Award
1985   <www.iema-ia.org/itaindex.html>   6-9

SPONSOR: Iowa Educational Media Association

PURPOSE: To encourage students to read more books; to aid students in choosing good books; to provide common ground among teachers, parents, and students for conversation about books and authors; and to give recognition to authors who write books for early teens.

SELECTION CRITERIA: Books chosen for the list must have been published within the last three years; may be fiction or nonfiction; should represent a wide range of subjects and reading levels. Previous *Iowa Teen Award* winners are excluded, as are books in a series, books without positive reviews in at least one major reviewing periodical, and novelizations of movies or TV programs.

VOTING: Students must read or hear at least two books from the list to be eligible to vote.

1985	6-9	*Tiger Eyes* by Judy Blume
1986	6-9	*When We First Met* by Norma Fox Mazer
1987	6-9	*You Shouldn't Have to Say Goodbye* by Patricia Hermes
1988	6-9	*Abby, My Love* by Hadley Irwin
1989	6-9	*The Other Side of Dark* by Joan Lowery Nixon
1990	6-9	*Hatchet* by Gary Paulsen
1991	6-9	*Silver* by Norma Fox Mazer
1992	6-9	*Don't Look Behind You* by Lois Duncan
1993	6-9	*The Face on the Milk Carton* by Caroline Cooney
1994	6-9	*Ryan White: My Own Story* by Ryan White
1995	6-9	*Jurassic Park* by Michael Crichton
1996	6-9	*Whatever Happened to Janie?* by Caroline Cooney
1997	6-9	*Harris and Me: A Summer Remembered* by Gary Paulsen
1998	6-9	*Brian's Winter* by Gary Paulsen
1999	6-9	*Crash* by Jerry Spinelli
2000	6-9	*Ella Enchanted* by Gail Carson Levine
2001	6-9	*Annie's Baby* by Beatrice Sparks
2002	6-9	*The Transall Saga* by Gary Paulsen
2003	6-9	*Stargirl* by Jerry Spinelli

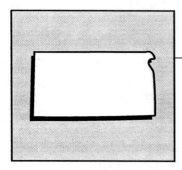

KANSAS

William Allen White Children's Book Award

1953   <www.emporia.edu/libsv/
wawbookaward/>   3-5, 6-8

SPONSOR: The award was established by Ruth Garver Gagliardo and is administered by Emporia State University.

PURPOSE: To introduce children to a variety of quality books, to celebrate reading, and to honor imaginative authors.

NAME ORIGIN: To honor the memory of one of the state's most distinguished citizens, William Allen White, editor of the *Emporia Gazette*, founder of the Progressive Party, and author.

SELECTION CRITERIA: To be eligible for inclusion, a book must have been first published in English in the United States, Canada, or Mexico within the calendar year immediately preceding the year when the lists are selected. Only books by authors who reside in the United States, Canada, or Mexico are eligible. Fiction, poetry, and nonfiction are eligible. Textbooks, anthologies, and translations are not eligible. Additional criteria in selecting titles include qualities of originality and vitality, clarity, factual accuracy in the case of nonfiction, sincerity of the author, and respect for the reader as well as acceptance by children.

VOTING: Students in the third through the eighth grades in Kansas schools are encouraged to read as many books as possible from the lists. When a student has read two books from either list, they are eligible to vote. Students may vote on both lists if they have read at least two books from each one.

1953	3-8	*Amos Fortune, Free Man* by Elizabeth Yates
1954	3-8	*Little Vic* by Doris Gates
1955	3-8	*Cherokee Bill, Oklahoma Pacer* by Jean Bailey
1956	3-8	*Brighty of the Grand Canyon* by Marguerite Henry
1957	3-8	*Daniel 'Coon* by Phoebe Erickson
1958	3-8	*White Falcon* by Elliott Arnold
1959	3-8	*Old Yeller* by Fred Gipson
1960	3-8	*Flaming Arrows* by William O. Steele

1961	3-8	*Henry Reed, Inc.* by Keith Robertson
1962	3-8	*The Helen Keller Story* by Catherine O. Peare
1963	3-8	*Island of the Blue Dolphins* by Scott O'Dell
1964	3-8	*The Incredible Journey* by Sheila Burnford
1965	3-8	*Bristle Face* by Zachary Ball
1966	3-8	*Rascal* by Sterling North
1967	3-8	*The Grizzly* by Annabel Johnson and Edgar Johnson
1968	3-8	*The Mouse and the Motorcycle* by Beverly Cleary
1969	3-8	*Henry Reed's Baby-sitting Service* by Keith Robertson
1970	3-8	*From the Mixed-Up Files of Mrs. Basil E. Frankweiler* by E. L. Konigsburg
1971	3-8	*Kavik, the Wolf Dog* by Walt Morey
1972	3-8	*Sasha, My Friend* by Barbara Corcoran
1973	3-8	*The Trumpet of the Swan* by E. B. White
1974	3-8	*Mrs. Frisby and the Rats of NIMH* by Robert O'Brien
1974	3-8	*The Headless Cupid* by Zilpha Keatley Snyder
1975	3-8	*Dominic* by William Steig
1976	3-8	*Socks* by Beverly Cleary
1977	3-8	*Harry Cat's Pet Puppy* by George Selden
1978	3-8	*The Great Christmas Kidnaping Caper* by Jean Van Leeuwen
1979	3-8	*Summer of the Monkeys* by Wilson Rawls
1980	3-8	*The Pinballs* by Betsy Byars
1981	3-8	*The Great Gilly Hopkins* by Katherine Paterson
1982	3-8	*The Magic of the Glits* by Carole S. Adler
1983	3-8	*Peppermints in the Parlor* by Barbara Brooks Wallace
1984	3-8	*A Light in the Attic* by Shel Silverstein
1985	3-8	*The Land I Lost: Adventures of a Boy in Vietnam* by Quang Nhuong Huynh
1986	3-8	*Daphne's Book* by Mary Downing Hahn
1987	3-8	*The War With Grandpa* by Robert Kimmel Smith
1988	3-8	*Cracker Jackson* by Betsy Byars
1989	3-8	*On My Honor* by Marion Dane Bauer
1990	3-8	*Hatchet* by Gary Paulsen
1991	3-8	*Beauty* by Bill Wallace
1992	3-8	*The Doll in the Garden: A Ghost Story* by Mary Downing Hahn
1993	3-8	*Maniac Magee* by Jerry Spinelli
1994	3-8	*Shiloh* by Phyllis Reynolds Naylor
1995	3-8	*The Man Who Loved Clowns* by June Rae Wood
1996	3-8	*The Giver* by Lois Lowry
1997	3-8	*Time for Andrew: A Ghost Story* by Mary Downing Hahn
1998	3-8	*Mick Harte Was Here* by Barbara Park
1999	3-8	*Frindle* by Andrew Clements

2000	3-8	*White Water* by P. J. Petersen
2001	3-5	*The Ghost of Fossil Glen* by Cynthia DeFelice
	6-8	*Holes* by Louis Sachar
2002	3-5	*The Landry News* by Andrew Clements
	6-8	*Bud, Not Buddy* by Christopher Paul Curtis
2003	3-5	*Because of Winn-Dixie* by Kate DiCamillo
	6-8	*Dovey Coe* by Frances O'Roark Dowell

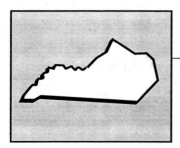

KENTUCKY

Kentucky Bluegrass Award
1983   <www.kyreading.org>   K-2, 3-5, 6-8, 9-12

SPONSOR: Kentucky Reading Association

PURPOSE: To encourage the students of Kentucky in kindergarten through twelfth grade to read quality children's literature.

NAME ORIGIN: Named after the state nickname—Bluegrass State.

SELECTION CRITERIA: Any adult may nominate books for the list with Kentucky teachers and librarians particularly encouraged to participate. Books published during the three years preceding the award year may be nominated. All books nominated should be of interest to students in kindergarten through twelfth grade. The most recent Caldecott, Newbery, and other award winning titles are not automatically included on the list. Titles previously included on a list will not be eligible for the current list.

VOTING: Students rate each book they read from the list. Ratings are Great, Good, OK, Not Too Bad, Bad.

1983	K-3	*Jumanji* by Chris Van Allsburg
1984	K-3	*Move Over, Twerp* by Martha Alexander
1985	K-3	*Angelina Ballerina* by Katherine Holabird. Helen Craig, ill.
1986	K-3	*Badger's Parting Gifts* by Susan Varley
1987	K-3	*Polar Express* by Chris Van Allsburg
1988	K-3	*Hey, Al!* by Arthur Yorinks. Richard Egielski, ill.
	4-8	*Who Needs a Bratty Brother?* by Linda Gondosch
1989	K-3	*The Wolf's Chicken Stew* by Keiko Kasza
	4-8	*Class Clown* by Johanna Hurwitz
1990	K-3	*The Lady With the Alligator Purse* by Nadine Bernard Westcott
	4-8	*The Stranger* by Chris Van Allsburg
1991	K-3	*Chicka Chicka Boom Boom* by Bill Martin, Jr. and John Archambault. Lois Ehlert, ill.
	4-8	*The Butterfly Jar* by Jeff Moss
1992	K-3	*Basket* by George Ella Lyon. Mary Szilagyi, ill.
	4-8	*Something Big Has Been Here* by Jack Prelutsky

1993	K-3	*Tuesday* by David Wiesner
	4-8	*Brother Eagle, Sister Sky: A Message from Chief Seattle* by Chief Seattle
1994	K-3	*Pigs Aplenty, Pigs Galore!* by David McPhail
	4-8	*Bob and Jack: A Boy and His Yak* by Jeff Moss
1995	K-3	*The Cow Who Wouldn't Come Down* by Paul Brett Johnson
	4-8	*The Hero of Bremen* by Margaret Hodges
1996	K-3	*Harvey Potter's Balloon Farm* by Jerdine Nolen. Mark Buehner, ill.
	4-8	*The Christmas of the Reddle Moon* by J. Patrick Lewis
1997	K-3	*Officer Buckle and Gloria* by Peggy Rathman
	4-8	*Piggie Pie* by Margie Palatini
1998	K-3	*Lilly's Purple Plastic Purse* by Kevin Henkes
	4-8	*Minty: A Story of Young Harriet Tubman* by Alan Schroeder
1999	K-3	*A Perfect Pork Stew* by Paul Brett Johnson
	4-8	*Christopher Changes His Name* by Itah Sadu and Roy Condy
2000	K-3	*Hooway for Wodney Wat!* by Helen Lester. Lynn Munsinger, ill.
	4-8	*Smoky Mountain Rose: An Appalachian Cinderella* by Alan Schroeder
2001	K-2	*Don't Need Friends* by Carolyn Crimi. Lynn Munsinger, ill.
	3-5	*The Babe and I* by David Adler
	6-8	*Secrets of the Mummies: Uncovering the Bodies of Ancient Egyptians* by Shelley Tanaka
	9-12	*Speak* by Laurie Halse Anderson
2002	K-2	*One Lucky Girl* by George Ella Lyon. Irene Trivas, ill.
	(3-5)	*So You Want to Be President?* by Judith St. George
	6-8	*Stuck in Neutral* by Terry Trueman
	9-12	*Monster* by Walter Dean Myers
2003	K-2	*Hoodwinked* by Arthur Howard
	(3-5)	*Albert* by Donna Jo Napoli
	6-8	*Knocked Out By My Nunga-Nungas: Further, Further Confessions of Georgia Nicolson* by Louise Rennison
	9-12	*The Brimstone Journals* by Ron Koertge

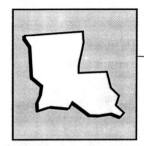

LOUISIANA

Louisiana Young Readers' Choice Award
2000
<http://test.state.lib.la.us/la_dyn_templ.cfm?doc_id=83> 3-5

SPONSOR: State Library of Louisiana, Louisiana Center for the Book, underwritten by the Hibernia National Bank.

PURPOSE: To foster a love of reading in the children of Louisiana and to give them the opportunity to participate in the selection of books worthy of receiving an award for literary excellence. The award seeks to excite children about reading by encouraging them to read and compare high quality books, and to honor the authors of outstanding books for children.

SELECTION CRITERIA: Considerations for inclusion on the list will include literary quality, effectiveness of expression, creativity, imagination, reading enjoyment, reading level, interest level, genre representation, gender representation, racial diversity, diversity of social, political, economic or religious viewpoints, and availability. The award will be limited to books published three years before the award. This must be the original U.S. copyright date, not a reprint date or copyright date of the paperback, unless the paperback edition is the original edition. The books must be in print. The author does not have to be an American citizen, but the book must be published in the United States. Both fiction and nonfiction books will be considered for the award. The list contains 15 titles.

VOTING: Each child may vote for his or her favorite book at participating schools and public libraries. The child must reside in Louisiana, be in grade three, four or five (or equivalent), and must read or hear at least three of the titles on the list. Each child may vote only once.

2000	3-5	*Verdi* by Janell Cannon
2001	3-5	*Harry Potter and the Sorcerer's Stone* by J. K. Rowling
2002	3-5	*Weslandia* by Paul Fleischman
2003	3-5	*My Dog, My Hero* by Betsy Byars and Betsy Duffey

MAINE

Maine Student Book Award
1991   <www.windham.lib.me.us/msba.htm>   4-8

SPONSOR: Maine Library Association, Maine Association of School Libraries, Maine Reading Association

PURPOSE: To expand literary horizons of students in grades four through eight by encouraging them to read, evaluate, and enjoy a selection of new books and to choose a statewide favorite.

NAME ORIGIN: A committee was formed to encourage young readers in Maine to explore current literature and to have their voices heard. Therefore, the award was named for them.

SELECTION CRITERIA: Books must have been published the previous year; must be original or, if traditional in origin, the result of individual research. All forms of writing are eligible for consideration including fiction and nonfiction, short stories, drama, and poetry. Books should have young readers as their intended audience, display respect for children's understanding, ability, and appreciation, and be appropriate for students in grades four through eight.

VOTING: Each student who has read at least three books from the list may cast one vote.

1991	4-8	*Number the Stars* by Lois Lowry
1992	4-8	*Fudge-A-Mania* by Judy Blume
1993	4-8	*Shiloh* by Phyllis Reynolds Naylor
1994	4-8	*The Stinky Cheese Man and Other Fairly Stupid Tales* by Jon Scieszka
1995	4-8	*The Giver* by Lois Lowry
1996	4-8	*Pink and Say* by Patricia Polacco
1997	4-8	*Math Curse* by Jon Scieszka
1998	4-8	*Falling Up* by Shel Silverstein
1999	4-8	*Ella Enchanted* by Gail Carson Levine
2000	4-8	*Holes* by Louis Sachar
2001	4-8	*Harry Potter and the Prisoner of Azkaban* by J. K. Rowling
2002	4-8	*Because of Winn-Dixie* by Kate DiCamillo
2003	4-8	*Love That Dog* by Sharon Creech

MARYLAND

Maryland Black-Eyed Susan Book Award
1992 <www.tcps.k12.md.us/memo/besall.
html> K-12 Picture Book, 4-6, 6-9, 9-12

SPONSOR: Maryland Educational Media Organization

PURPOSE: To promote lifelong reading habits by encouraging students to read and enjoy quality, contemporary literature which broadens understanding of the human experience.

NAME ORIGIN: Named after the state flower—Black-Eyed Susan.

SELECTION CRITERIA: Books may be fiction or nonfiction; have a copyright date of the current year or one of the preceding three years and be listed in the current *Books in Print*. Each title selected should have received positive reviews from appropriate professional journals.

VOTING: To participate, students must read or hear a minimum of eight of the 15 picture books nominated. Based on the premise that picture books are for everyone, there are no grade level restrictions. To participate, students in grades four through six and grades six through nine must read or hear a minimum of three of the nominated books on the lists. To participate at the high school level, students read a minimum of three of the nominated books.

1992	K-12	*The True Story of the Three Little Pigs* by Jon Scieszka. Lane Smith, ill.
	4-6	*Matilda* by Roald Dahl
1993	K-12	*The Araboolies of Liberty Street* by Sam Swope. Barry Root, ill.
	4-6	*Fudge-A-Mania* by Judy Blume
	6-9	*The Silver Kiss* by Annette Curtis Klause
1994	K-12	*Trouble With Trolls* by Jan Brett
	4-6	*Jeremy Thatcher, Dragon Hatcher* by Bruce Coville
	6-9	*Stepping on the Cracks* by Mary Downing Hahn
1995	K-12	*Go Away, Big Green Monster!* by Ed Emberley
	4-6	*Fourth Grade Rats* by Jerry Spinelli
	6-9	*The Giver* by Lois Lowry
1996	K-12	*Harvey Potter's Balloon Farm* by Jerdine Nolen. Mark Buehner, ill.

	4-6	*Ghosts Don't Get Goose Bumps* by Elvira Woodruff
	6-9	*Night Terrors* by Jim Murphy
1997	K-12	*Soap! Soap! Don't Forget the Soap!* by Tom Birdseye. Andrew Glass, ill.
	4-6	*Time for Andrew: A Ghost Story* by Mary Downing Hahn
	6-9	*The Name of the Game Was Murder* by Joan Lowery Nixon
1998	K-12	*Piggie Pie* by Margie Palatini. Howard Fine, ill.
	4-6	*The 13th Floor: A Ghost Story* by Sid Fleischman
	6-9	*Running Out of Time* by Margaret Peterson Haddix
1999	K-12	*Just Another Ordinary Day* by Rod Clement
	4-6	*Frindle* by Andrew Clements
	6-9	*Don't You Dare Read This, Mrs. Dunphrey* by Margaret Peterson Haddix
2000	K-12	*A Bad Case of Stripes* by David Shannon
	4-6	*101 Ways to Bug Your Parents* by Lee Wardlaw
	6-9	*Ella Enchanted* by Gail Carson Levine
	9-12	*Danger Zone* by David Klass
2001	K-12	*Rotten Teeth* by Laura Simms. David Catrow, ill.
	4-6	*The 6th Grade Nickname Game* by Gordon Korman
	6-9	*Holes* by Louis Sachar
	9-12	*Someone Like You* by Sarah Dessen
	9-12	*The Killer's Cousin* by Nancy Werlin
2002	K-12	*Click, Clack, Moo: Cows That Type* by Doreen Cronin. Betsy Lewin, ill.
	4-6	*Because of Winn-Dixie* by Kate DiCamillo
	6-9	*There's a Dead Person Following My Sister Around* by Vivian Vande Velde
	9-12	*If You Come Softly* by Jacqueline Woodson
2003	K-12	*The Web Files* by Margie Palatini. Richard Egielski, ill.
	4-6	*Cody Unplugged* by Betsy Duffey
	6-9	*Define Normal: A Novel* by Julie Anne Peters
	9-12	*The Sisterhood of the Traveling Pants* by Ann Brashares

MARYLAND

Maryland Children's Book Award
1988   <www.somd.lib.md.us/mcbap/welcome.
htm>   K-2 (Primary), 3-5 (Intermediate), 6-8
(Middle School)

SPONSOR: State of Maryland International Reading Association Council

PURPOSE: To foster Maryland students' interest in quality literature and to honor the books chosen by Maryland students.

SELECTION CRITERIA: Books nominated must be appropriate for kindergarten through grade six; should have literary value; and must be in print. Award-winning books are not eligible. Only primary titles published in the last five years are eligible, and intermediate and middle level titles must be published within the last 10 years. Only one title per author may be nominated per year and authors must be living in the United States at the time of nomination. Once nominated, a title will be excluded from subsequent lists and the winning author will be excluded from nomination the following year.

VOTING: To be eligible to vote, students at the primary level must read or hear at least five of the books. Students at the intermediate and middle school levels must read or hear at least three of the books.

1988	3-5	*Cracker Jackson* by Betsy Byars
1989	3-5	*Switcharound* by Lois Lowry
1990	3-5	*The Haunting of Cabin 13* by Kristi Holl
1991	3-5	*The Doll in the Garden: A Ghost Story* by Mary Downing Hahn
1992	3-5	*My Teacher is an Alien* by Bruce Coville
1993	K-2	*Two Bad Ants* by Chris Van Allsburg
	3-5	*Grasshopper Summer* by Ann Turner
1994	K-2	*High-Wire Henry* by Mary Calhoun. Erick Ingraham, ill.
	3-5	*Danger in Quicksand Swamp* by Bill Wallace
	6-8	*Sniper* by Theodore Taylor
1995	K-2	*Hurricane City* by Sarah Weeks. James Warhola, ill.
	3-5	*The Boys Start the War* by Phyllis Reynolds Naylor
	6-8	*Flight #116 Is Down* by Caroline Cooney
1996	K-2	*Dogs Don't Wear Sneakers* by Laura Numeroff. Joe Mathieu, ill.

	3-5	*Time for Andrew: A Ghost Story* by Mary Downing Hahn
	6-8	*Randall's Wall* by Carol Fenner
1997	K-2	*Cadillac* by Charles Temple. Lynne Lockhart, ill.
	3-5	*Poison Ivy and Eyebrow Wigs* by Bonnie Pryor
	6-8	*Freak the Mighty* by Rodman Philbrick
1998	K-2	*Tops and Bottoms* by Janet Stevens
	3-5	*Poppy* by Avi
	6-8	*Stranded* by Ben Mikaelsen
1999	K-2	*Verdi* by Janell Cannon
	3-5	*Santa Paws* by Nicholas Edwards
	6-8	*Crash* by Jerry Spinelli
2000	K-2	*The Polar Bear Son: An Inuit Tale* by Lydia Dabcovich
	3-5	*My Life As a Fifth-Grade Comedian* by Elizabeth Levy
	6-8	*Tangerine* by Edward Bloor
2001	K-2	*Hooway for Wodney Wat!* by Helen Lester. Lynn Munsinger, ill.
	3-5	*The Ghost of Fossil Glen* by Cynthia DeFelice
	6-8	*Fire Pony* by Rodman Philbrick
2002	K-2	*Bark, George* by Jules Feiffer
	3-5	*The Doll People* by Ann M. Martin and Laura Godwin
	6-8	*Jackie and Me: A Baseball Card Adventure* by Dan Gutman
2003	K-2	*A Bad Case of Stripes* by David Shannon
	3-5	*Joey Pigza Swallowed the Key* by Jack Gantos
	6-8	*As Ever, Gordy* by Mary Downing Hahn

MASSACHUSETTS

Massachusetts Children's Book Award
1976 <www.salemstate.edu/education/mcba/> 4-6

SPONSOR: Salem State College

SELECTION CRITERIA: Participating teachers and librarians along with publishers nominate titles for the program with the following criteria: literary quality, variety of genres, representation of diverse cultural groups, reader appeal, and books published within a five-year period before the award year. The list contains 25 books.

VOTING: Students must read or hear at least five books from the list to be eligible to vote.

1976	4-6	*How to Eat Fried Worms* by Thomas Rockwell
1977	4-6	*Tales of a Fourth Grade Nothing* by Judy Blume
1978	4-6	*Mrs. Frisby and the Rats of NIMH* by Robert O'Brien
1979	4-6	*The Cricket in Times Square* by George Selden
1980	4-6	*Chocolate Fever* by Robert Kimmel Smith
1981	4-6	*The Great Gilly Hopkins* by Katherine Paterson
1982	4-6	*James and the Giant Peach: A Children's Story* by Roald Dahl
1983	4-6	*Tales of a Fourth Grade Nothing* by Judy Blume
1984	4-6	*Charlotte's Web* by E. B. White
1985	4-6	*Nothing's Fair in Fifth Grade* by Barthe DeClements
1986	4-6	*Dear Mr. Henshaw* by Beverly Cleary
1987	4-6	*Where the Red Fern Grows: The Story of Two Dogs and a Boy* by Wilson Rawls
1988	4-6	*The Indian in the Cupboard* by Lynne Reid Banks
1989	4-6	*The Chocolate Touch* by Patrick Catling
1991	4-6	*There's a Boy in the Girls' Bathroom* by Louis Sachar
1992	4-6	*Matilda* by Roald Dahl
1993	4-6	*Maniac Magee* by Jerry Spinelli
1994	4-6	*Shiloh* by Phyllis Reynolds Naylor
1995	4-6	*Hatchet* by Gary Paulsen
1996	4-6	*Blubber* by Judy Blume
1997	4-6	*Wayside School Gets a Little Stranger* by Louis Sachar
1998	4-6	*Crash* by Jerry Spinelli
1999	4-6	*Frindle* by Andrew Clements
2000	4-6	*Harry Potter and the Sorcerer's Stone* by J. K. Rowling

2001 4-6 *Holes* by Louis Sachar
2002 4-6 *Because of Winn-Dixie* by Kate DiCamillo
2003 4-6 *Artemis Fowl* by Eoin Colfer

MICHIGAN

Great Lakes' Great Books Award
1989   <www.michiganreading.org/greatbooks/index.html>   K-1, 2-3, 4-5, 6-8

SPONSOR: Michigan Reading Association

PURPOSE: To encourage children to read more and better books and to read discriminately.

NAME ORIGIN: A new name was chosen in 2003. Teachers around the state sent in entries and the committee chose the winner. The former name was *Michigan Reading Association Readers' Choice Award*.

SELECTION CRITERIA: Books must have been published within the past two years when nominated. Content (language and subject) and appeal of the books should be appropriate to the grade ranges of the award. Eight books appear on the list for each grade category.

VOTING: Students read at least five titles on the list for their grade level before voting.

1989	K-2	*Polar Express* by Chris Van Allsburg
	3-5	*Superfudge* by Judy Blume
	6-8	*The BFG* by Roald Dahl
1991	K-2	*Polar Express* by Chris Van Allsburg
	3-5	*The Indian in the Cupboard* by Lynne Reid Banks
	6-8	*The Indian in the Cupboard* by Lynne Reid Banks
1993	K-2	*The Very Quiet Cricket* by Eric Carle
	3-5	*Fudge-A-Mania* by Judy Blume
	6-8	*Scary Stories 3: More Tales to Chill Your Bones* by Alvin Schwartz
1996	K-2	*The Rainbow Fish* by Marcus Pfister
	3-5	*Monster Blood II* by R. L. Stine
	6-8	*The Giver* by Lois Lowry
2000	K-2	*The Brave Little Parrot* by Susan Gaber
	3-5	*Stay!: Keeper's Story* by Lois Lowry
	6-8	*Tangerine* by Edward Bloor
2002	K-1	*Bark, George* by Jules Feiffer
	2-3	*The Legend of Mackinac Island* by Kathy-Jo Wargin

	4-5	*Star in the Storm* by Joan Hiatt Harlow
	6-8	*When Zachary Beaver Came to Town* by Kimberly Willis Holt
2003	K-1	*Baby Beebee Bird* by Diane Redfield Massie. Steven Kellogg, ill.
	2-3	*Adopted By an Owl* by Robbyn Smith van Frankenhuyzen
	4-5	*Fever, 1793* by Laurie Halse Anderson
	6-8	*No More Dead Dogs* by Gordon Korman

MINNESOTA

Maud Hart Lovelace Book Award
1980   <www.isd77.k12.mn.us/lovelace/ lovelace.
html>   3-5 (Division I), 6-8 (Division II)

SPONSOR: Minnesota Youth Reading Awards, Minnesota Library Association, Minnesota Reading Association, Minnesota Educational Media Organization

PURPOSE: To encourage recreational reading among school-age children.

NAME ORIGIN: Maud Hart Lovelace was a famous author, born and raised in Minnesota. She loved reading and wrote stories from the time she was young. "I cannot remember back to the year in which I did not consider myself a writer." It is because of her creativity and enduring work that Maud Hart Lovelace is honored through a children's book award.

SELECTION CRITERIA: The books must be available in paperback and have a copyright date within the last five years. The author must be living in North America and may not have works included on the final list for two consecutive years. The books must be fiction, cannot be classified as picture books, or be part of a formula series. Titles may include a variety of genres including stories of regional interest or stories by a Minnesota author. Titles selected will reflect cultural, ethnic, and gender diversity as well as a fair depiction of any characters with disabilities. The interest levels for the nominated titles range from third through eighth grade. YA titles will have a review to be considered for nomination, and any title nominated which contains mature subject matter will receive a "Mature Readers" designation. Twelve books are nominated for each grade division.

VOTING: Students are encouraged to read at least three of the nominated books to be eligible to vote.

1980	3-8	*Summer of the Monkeys* by Wilson Rawls
1981	3-8	*The Pinballs* by Betsy Byars
1982	3-8	*The Best Christmas Pageant Ever* by Barbara Robinson
1983	3-8	*It Can't Hurt Forever* by Marilyn Singer
1984	3-8	*Nothing's Fair in Fifth Grade* by Barthe DeClements
1985	3-8	*Skinnybones* by Barbara Park

1986	3-8	*Zucchini* by Barbara Dana
1987	3-8	*Stone Fox* by John Gardiner
1988	3-8	*Night of the Twisters* by Ivy Ruckman
1989	3-8	*Eating Ice Cream With a Werewolf* by Phyllis Green
1990	3-8	*Wait Till Helen Comes* by Mary Downing Hahn
1991	3-8	*Hatchet* by Gary Paulsen
1992	3-8	*This Island Isn't Big Enough for the Four of Us* by Gery Greer and Bob Ruddick
1993	3-8	*The Dead Man in Indian Creek* by Mary Downing Hahn
1994	3-8	*38 Weeks Till Summer Vacation* by Mona Kerby
1995	3-8	*Nightmare Mountain* by Peg Kehret
1996	3-8	*Cages* by Peg Kehret
1997	3-5	*The Summer I Shrank My Grandmother* by Elvira Woodruff
	6-8	*The Devil's Arithmetic* by Jane Yolen
1998	3-5	*Mick Harte Was Here* by Barbara Park
	6-8	*Mick Harte Was Here* by Barbara Park
1999	3-5	*Frindle* by Andrew Clements
	6-8	*Crash* by Jerry Spinelli
2000	3-5	*Danger in the Desert* by Terri Fields
	6-8	*Tangerine* by Edward Bloor
2001	3-5	*The Million Dollar Shot* by Dan Gutman
	6-8	*Among the Hidden* by Margaret Peterson Haddix
2002	3-5	*Silverwing* by Kenneth Oppel
	6-8	*Trapped Between the Lash and the Gun: A Boy's Journey* by Arvella Whitmore
2003	3-5	*The Ghost of Fossil Glen* by Cynthia DeFelice
	6-8	*Dovey Coe* by Frances O'Roark Dowell

MISSISSIPPI

Mississippi Children's Book Award
1989   4-6

SPONSOR: University of Southern Mississippi, School of Library Service, de Grummond Collection. The award was only in existence for two years, 1989 and 1990. When three of the four organizers of the award left the university, the work to continue the award became too great for one person and the award was discontinued.

1989   4-6   *Class Clown* by Johanna Hurwitz
1990   4-6   *All About Sam* by Lois Lowry

MISSOURI

Gateway Award

2001   <http://maslonline.org/awards/books/Gateway/>   9-12

SPONSOR: Missouri Association of School Librarians

PURPOSE: To encourage Missouri young adults in grades nine through twelve to select and read quality literature that appeals to their needs, interests, and reading levels; to recognize and honor outstanding works in young adult literature; to develop a cooperative relationship between schools, libraries, and teens; to encourage the development of school and public library services to teens.

NAME ORIGIN: To symbolize that Missouri was the gateway to the west, and the book list is a gateway to reading.

SELECTION CRITERIA: Books should be appropriate and of interest to teenagers in grades nine through twelve; be written by an author living in the United States; be of literary value. Books should be published two years before nomination. Some consideration should be given to genre diversity, gender representation, range of reading level (avoiding elementary levels), racial diversity, and diversity of social, political, economic, and religious viewpoints. The list contains 15 titles.

VOTING: Students must read a minimum of three books from the list to be eligible to vote.

2001   9-12   *Someone Like You* by Sarah Dessen
2002   9-12   *A Walk to Remember* by Nicholas Sparks
2003   9-12   *Dreamland: A Novel* by Sarah Dessen

MISSOURI

Mark Twain Award

1972   <http://maslonline.org/awards/books/
MarkTwain/>   4-8

SPONSOR: Missouri Association of School Librarians

PURPOSE: To provide the children of Missouri with their very own source to enrich their lives through reading.

NAME ORIGIN: Named for the pen name of author Samuel Clemens, "Mark Twain."

SELECTION CRITERIA: The author must be a living United States author, and titles should have literary merit for the stated grade range.

VOTING: Missouri students in grades four through eight are eligible to vote for their favorite book if they have read or heard at least four of the titles on the list.

1972	4-8	*Sounder* by William Armstrong
1973	4-8	*Mrs. Frisby and the Rats of NIMH* by Robert O'Brien
1974	4-8	*It's a Mile From Here to Glory* by Robert C. Lee
1975	4-8	*How to Eat Fried Worms* by Thomas Rockwell
1976	4-8	*The Home Run Trick* by Scott Corbett
1977	4-8	*The Ghost on Saturday Night* by Sid Fleischman
1978	4-8	*Ramona the Brave* by Beverly Cleary
1979	4-8	*The Champion of Merrimack County* by Roger Drury
1980	4-8	*The Pinballs* by Betsy Byars
1981	4-8	*Soup for President* by Robert Newton Peck
1982	4-8	*The Boy Who Saw Bigfoot* by Marian T. Place
1983	4-8	*The Girl With the Silver Eyes* by Willo Davis Roberts
1984	4-8	*The Secret Life of the Underwear Champ* by Betty Miles
1985	4-8	*A Bundle of Sticks* by Pat Rhoads Mauser
1986	4-8	*The Dollhouse Murders* by Betty Ren Wright
1987	4-8	*The War With Grandpa* by Robert Kimmel Smith
1988	4-8	*Baby-Sitting is a Dangerous Job* by Willo Davis Roberts
1989	4-8	*The Sixth Grade Sleepover* by Eve Bunting
1990	4-8	*There's a Boy in the Girls' Bathroom* by Louis Sachar
1991	4-8	*All About Sam* by Lois Lowry

1992	4-8	*The Doll in the Garden: A Ghost Story* by Mary Downing Hahn
1993	4-8	*Maniac Magee* by Jerry Spinelli
1994	4-8	*Shiloh* by Phyllis Reynolds Naylor
1995	4-8	*The Man Who Loved Clowns* by June Rae Wood
1996	4-8	*The Ghosts of Mercy Manor* by Betty Ren Wright
1997	4-8	*Time for Andrew: A Ghost Story* by Mary Downing Hahn
1998	4-8	*Titanic Crossing* by Barbara Williams
1999	4-8	*Small Steps: The Year I Got Polio* by Peg Kehret
2000	4-8	*Saving Shiloh* by Phyllis Reynolds Naylor
2001	4-8	*Holes* by Louis Sachar
2002	4-8	*Dork in Disguise* by Carol Gorman
2003	4-8	*Because of Winn-Dixie* by Kate DiCamillo

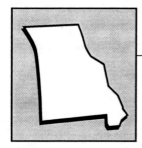

MISSOURI

Show Me Readers Award
1995   <http://maslonline.org/awards/books/
ShowMe/>   1-3

SPONSOR: Missouri Association of School Librarians

PURPOSE: To promote literature, literacy, and reading in Missouri elementary schools for grades one through three, and to promote recognition of authors and illustrators of books that are favorites of Missouri children in these grades.

NAME ORIGIN: Named after the state nickname—Show Me State.

SELECTION CRITERIA: The author must be a living United States author, and titles should have literary merit for the stated grade range.

VOTING: Children in grades one through three are eligible to vote for their favorite book if they read or hear a minimum of six books on the list.

1995	1-3	*Sukey and the Mermaid* by Robert D. San Souci. Brian Pinkney, ill.
1996	1-3	*Soap! Soap! Don't Forget the Soap!* by Tom Birdseye. Andrew Glass, ill.
1997	1-3	*My Rotten Redheaded Older Brother* by Patricia Polacco
1998	1-3	*Heart of a Tiger* by Marsha Diane Arnold. Jamichael Henterly, ill.
1999	1-3	*Duke, the Dairy Delight Dog* by Lisa Campbell Ernst
2000	1-3	*Verdi* by Janell Cannon
2001	1-3	*Raising Dragons* by Jerdine Nolen. Elise Primavera, ill.
2002	1-3	*Hooway for Wodney Wat!* by Helen Lester. Lynn Munsinger, ill.
2003	1-3	*Go Home! The True Story of James the Cat* by Libby Phillips Meggs

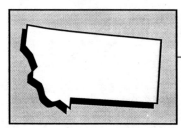

MONTANA

See Pacific Northwest

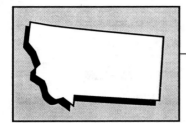

MONTANA

Treasure State Award
1991 K-3

SPONSOR: Missoula Public Library, Missoula County Schools

PURPOSE: To begin the analytical process of comparing one book to another and to prepare students in Montana to continue on with this process with the Pacific Northwest Library Association's Young Reader's Choice Award, which is for grades four through twelve.

NAME ORIGIN: A contest. A third grader from Helena, Montana submitted the winning name.

SELECTION CRITERIA: Books must be published within five years of the voting year. Suggestions are received from teachers, librarians, students, and parents.

VOTING: Students must read or listen to all five of the nominated titles to be eligible to vote.

1991	K-3	*The Dragon Nanny* by C. L. G. Martin
1992	K-3	*Cock-a-Doodle Dudley* by Bill Peet
1993	K-3	*High-Wire Henry* by Mary Calhoun. Erick Ingraham, ill.
1994	K-3	*Trouble With Trolls* by Jan Brett
1995	K-3	*Coyote Steals the Blanket: A Ute Tale* by Janet Stevens
1996	K-3	*Zomo the Rabbit: A Trickster Tale from South Africa* by Gerald McDermott
1997	K-3	*Three Cheers for Tacky* by Helen Lester. Lynn Munsinger, ill.
1998	K-3	*The Girl Who Wanted to Hunt: A Siberian Tale* by Emery Bernhard. Durga Bernhard, ill.
1999	K-3	*A Bad Case of Stripes* by David Shannon
2000	K-3	*Punia and the King of the Sharks: A Hawaiian Folktale* by Lee Wardlaw. Felipe Davalos, ill.
2001	K-3	*Akiak: A Tale from the Iditarod* by Robert J. Blake.
2002	K-3	*Enemy Pie* by Derek Munson. Tara Calahan King, ill.
2003	K-3	*Ignis* by Gina Wilson. P. J. Lynch, ill.

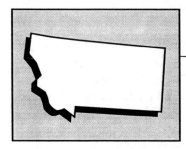

NEBRASKA

Golden Sower Award
1981   <www.state.ne.us/home/NLA/golden/
sower.htm>   K-3, 4-6, 6-9 (Young Adult)

SPONSOR: Nebraska Library Association's School, Children, and Young People Section

PURPOSE: The award's sponsors hope the program will sow seeds which stimulate children's thinking, introduce different types of literature, encourage independent reading, increase library skills, and foster an appreciation for excellence in writing and illustrating.

NAME ORIGIN: Named after a statue. On top of the Nebraska State Capitol in Lincoln stands a 19,000 pound, bronze statue known as the Sower. He stands, barefoot and without hat, sowing seeds in the most primitive manner. He is symbolic of the state of Nebraska as a major agricultural state. He is not merely sowing seeds of grain, but something much greater. He is the symbol of the intrinsic principles of living, a sower of the seeds of life, which will bring into being a finer life for the future. The Sower was chosen as the symbol of Nebraska's children's choice literary award for similar reasons. It is hoped that the Golden Sower Award will sow the seeds which will help to develop an appreciation for excellence in writing and beauty in illustrations among Nebraska's children that will stay with them all of their lives. Whether for pleasure or information, the reading of quality literature will enrich lives and sow seeds for a finer future life.

SELECTION CRITERIA: The books nominated should exhibit literary and artistic merit. Eligible titles must have been published within three years preceding the current year; should reflect an equitable consideration for a culturally diverse society; must be in print at the time of nomination; award winners are not eligible for nomination. The authors and illustrators should be living in the United States at the time of nomination and only one title of any one author or illustrator will be included on the lists. Authors and illustrators represented on the final lists may be repeated, but not individual titles. The winning author and illustrator are excluded from competition the following year. The list contains 10 books for each category.

VOTING: Children must read or hear four titles to be eligible to vote.

1981	4-6	*Bunnicula: A Rabbit Tale of Mystery* by James Howe
1982	4-6	*Yours Till Niagara Falls, Abby* by Jane O'Connor
1983	K-3	*Cloudy With a Chance of Meatballs* by Judi Barrett. Ron Barrett, ill.
	4-6	*Superfudge* by Judy Blume
1984	K-3	*Miss Nelson Is Back* by Harry Allard. James Marshall, ill.
	4-6	*Nothing's Fair in Fifth Grade* by Barthe DeClements
1985	K-3	*Round Trip* by Ann Jonas
	4-6	*A Dog Called Kitty* by Bill Wallace
1986	K-3	*Peabody* by Rosemary Wells
	4-6	*Night of the Twisters* by Ivy Ruckman
1987	K-3	*Miss Nelson Has a Field Day* by Harry Allard. James Marshall, ill.
	4-6	*The War With Grandpa* by Robert Kimmel Smith
1988	K-3	*Don't Touch My Room* by Patricia Lakin
	4-6	*Sixth Grade Can Really Kill You* by Barthe DeClements
1989	K-3	*Piggins* by Jane Yolen. Jane Dyer, ill.
	4-6	*Ferret in the Bedroom, Lizards in the Fridge* by Bill Wallace
1990	K-3	*The Magic School Bus at the Waterworks* by Joanna Cole. Bruce Degan, ill.
	4-6	*Wait Till Helen Comes* by Mary Downing Hahn
1991	K-3	*Tacky the Penguin* by Helen Lester. Lynn Munsinger, ill.
	4-6	*There's a Boy in the Girls' Bathroom* by Louis Sachar
1992	K-3	*The Talking Eggs: A Folktale from the American South* by Robert D. San Souci. Jerry Pinkney, ill.
	4-6	*Is Anybody There?* by Eve Bunting
1993	K-3	*Riptide* by Frances Ward Weller. Robert J. Blake, ill.
	4-6	*Nightmare Mountain* by Peg Kehret
	6-9	*Whispers From the Dead* by Joan Lowery Nixon
1994	K-3	*The Rough-Face Girl* by Rafe Martin. David Shannon, ill.
	4-6	*Stepping on the Cracks* by Mary Downing Hahn
	6-9	*Flight #116 Is Down* by Caroline Cooney
1995	K-3	*Martha Speaks* by Susan Meddaugh
	4-6	*Rescue Josh McGuire* by Ben Mikaelsen
	6-9	*The Giver* by Lois Lowry
1996	K-3	*Soap! Soap! Don't Forget the Soap!* by Tom Birdseye. Andrew Glass, ill.
	4-6	*The Grand Escape* by Phyllis Reynolds Naylor
	6-9	*Heart of a Champion* by Carl Deuker
1997	K-3	*John Henry* by Julius Lester

	4-6	*The Best School Year Ever* by Barbara Robinson
	6-9	*Freak the Mighty* by Rodman Philbrick
1998	K-3	*The Toll-Bridge Troll* by Patricia Rae Wolff. Kimberly Bulcken Root, ill.
	4-6	*Titanic Crossing* by Barbara Williams
	6-9	*Danger Zone* by David Klass
1999	K-3	*Rugby and Rosie* by Nan Parson Rossiter
	4-6	*Shiloh Season* by Phyllis Reynolds Naylor
	6-9	*The True Colors of Caitlynne Jackson* by Carol Lynch Williams
2000	K-3	*No Such Thing* by Jackie French Koller
	4-6	*Jaguar* by Roland Smith
	6-9	*Don't You Dare Read This, Mrs. Dunphrey* by Margaret Peterson Haddix
2001	K-3	*Bubba, the Cowboy Prince* by Helen Ketteman
	4-6	*The Ghost of Fossil Glen* by Cynthia DeFelice
	6-9	*The Haunting* by Joan Lowery Nixon
2002	K-3	*The Grannyman* by Judith Byron Schachner
	4-6	*The Ghost of Lizard Light* by Elvira Woodruff
	6-9	*The Transall Saga* by Gary Paulsen
2003	K-3	*Bedhead* by Margie Palatini
	4-6	*Because of Winn-Dixie* by Kate DiCamillo
	6-9	*Night Hoops* by Carl Deuker

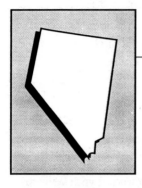

NEVADA

Nevada Young Readers' Award

1988 <www.nevadalibraries.org/Divisions/
NYRA/index.html> K-2 (Picture Books), 3-5
(Young Reader), 6-8 (Intermediate), 9-12 (Young
Adult)

SPONSOR: Nevada Library Association, Nevada Department of Education

PURPOSE: To encourage the children in Nevada to improve their reading skills by reading from the best modern children's literature; to honor outstanding works in children's literature at all reading/interest levels; to encourage the love of reading and develop lifelong reading habits.

SELECTION CRITERIA: A book must appeal to the age group for which the nomination is made; be a title most often read or requested by young readers; and be published in the United States within the last three years.

VOTING: In order to vote, each student must read or hear the required number of titles in a particular category. Students vote once in each category for which they are qualified and may vote in more than one category.

1988	K-3	*Polar Express* by Chris Van Allsburg
	4-8	*Sixth Grade Can Really Kill You* by Barthe DeClements
1989	K-3	*If You Give a Mouse a Cookie* by Laura Numeroff. Felicia Bond, ill.
	4-8	*Baby-Sitting Is a Dangerous Job* by Willo Davis Roberts
	9-12	*Locked in Time* by Lois Duncan
1990	K-3	*Heckedy Peg* by Audrey Wood. Don Wood, ill.
	4-8	*There's a Boy in the Girls' Bathroom* by Louis Sachar
	9-12	*Experiment in Terror* by Bernal C. Payne, Jr.
1991	K-3	*We're Back! A Dinosaur's Story* by Hudson Talbott
	4-8	*My Teacher Is an Alien* by Bruce Coville
	9-12	*Princess Ashley* by Richard Peck
1992	K-3	*Call of the Wolves* by Jim Murphy. Mark Alan Weatherby, ill.
	4-8	*Matilda* by Roald Dahl
	9-12	*Whispers From the Dead* by Joan Lowery Nixon
1993	K-2	*The Dog Who Had Kittens* by Polly M. Robertus. Janet Stevens, ill.
	3-5	*Fudge-A-Mania* by Judy Blume
	6-8	*Maniac Magee* by Jerry Spinelli
	9-12	*Jurassic Park* by Michael Crichton

1994	K-2	*Look Out, Patrick!* by Paul Geraghty
	3-5	*Jeremy Thatcher, Dragon Hatcher* by Bruce Coville
	6-8	*Shiloh* by Phyllis Reynolds Naylor
	9-12	*Plague Year* by Stephanie Tolan
1995	K-2	*Moe the Dog in Tropical Paradise* by Diane Stanley. Elise Primavera, ill.
	3-5	*The Boys Start the War* by Phyllis Reynolds Naylor
	6-8	*Flight #116 Is Down* by Caroline Cooney
	9-12	*The Giver* by Lois Lowry
1996	K-2	*Coyote Steals the Blanket: A Ute Tale* by Janet Stevens
	3-5	*Junie B. Jones and Her Big Fat Mouth* by Barbara Park
	6-8	*The Name of the Game Was Murder* by Joan Lowery Nixon
	9-12	*Winners and Losers* by Stephen Hoffius
1997	K-2	*Harvey Potter's Balloon Farm* by Jerdine Nolen. Mark Buehner, ill.
	3-5	*Shape-Changer* by Bill Brittain
	6-8	*Loch: A Novel* by Paul Zindel
	9-12	*Shadow* by Joyce Sweeney
1998	K-2	*Secret Shortcut* by Mark Teague
	3-5	*Tarot Says Beware* by Betsy Byars
	6-8	*Crash* by Jerry Spinelli
	9-12	*Companions of the Night* by Vivian Vande Velde
1999	K-2	*Just Another Ordinary Day* by Rod Clement
	3-5	*Frindle* by Andrew Clements
	6-8	*The Doom Stone* by Paul Zindel
	9-12	*Tangerine* by Edward Bloor
2000	K-2	*John Willy and Freddy McGee* by Holly Meade
	3-5	*Harry Potter and the Sorcerer's Stone* by J. K. Rowling
	6-8	*Virtually Perfect* by Dan Gutman
	9-12	*Gallows Hill* by Lois Duncan
2001	K-2	*Mouse, Look Out!* by Judy Waite. Norma Burgin, ill.
	3-5	*Harry the Poisonous Centipede: A Story to Make You Squirm* by Lynne Reid Banks
	6-8	*Among the Hidden* by Margaret Peterson Haddix
	9-12	*Hero* by S. L. Rottman
2002	K-2	*Hooway for Wodney Wat!* by Helen Lester. Lynn Munsinger, ill.
	3-5	*Weird Stories From the Lonesome Café* by Judy Cox
	6-8	*Hostage* by Willo Davis Roberts
	9-12	*Burning Up* by Caroline Cooney
2003	K-2	*Hoodwinked* by Arthur Howard
	3-5	*The Bad Beginning* by Lemony Snicket
	6-8	*Zach's Lie* by Roland Smith
	9-12	*Touching Spirit Bear* by Ben Mikaelsen

NEW HAMPSHIRE

Great Stone Face Award
1980   <www.chilisnh.org/gsfaward.html>   4-6

SPONSOR: Children's Librarians of New Hampshire, a section of the New Hampshire Library Association

PURPOSE: To promote reading enjoyment among New Hampshire's fourth through sixth graders; to increase awareness of quality contemporary writing; and to allow children a chance to honor a favorite author.

NAME ORIGIN: Named after a natural rock formation found in the White Mountains.

SELECTION CRITERIA: Books must be published no more than three years from the current book award year. Books in a series are not considered unless those books will stand alone; no textbooks; Newbery books and books by foreign authors are considered.

VOTING: Students may read as many or as few books as they want.

1980	4-6	*Are You There, God? It's Me, Margaret* by Judy Blume
1981	4-6	*Superfudge* by Judy Blume
1982	4-6	*Tales of a Fourth Grade Nothing* by Judy Blume
1983	4-6	*The Mouse and the Motorcycle* by Beverly Cleary
1984	4-6	*Superfudge* by Judy Blume
1985	4-6	*Superfudge* by Judy Blume
1986	4-6	*Superfudge* by Judy Blume
1987	4-6	*Superfudge* by Judy Blume
1988	4-6	*Superfudge* by Judy Blume
1989	4-6	*Where the Red Fern Grows: The Story of Two Dogs and a Boy* by Wilson Rawls
1990	4-6	*Matilda* by Roald Dahl
1991	4-6	*The Secret of the Indian* by Lynne Reid Banks
1992	4-6	*Number the Stars* by Lois Lowry
1993	4-6	*Shiloh* by Phyllis Reynolds Naylor
1994	4-6	*Jeremy Thatcher, Dragon Hatcher* by Bruce Coville
1995	4-6	*Junie B. Jones and the Stupid, Smelly Bus* by Barbara Park
1996	4-6	*The Giver* by Lois Lowry
1997	4-6	*Math Curse* by Jon Scieszka

1998	4-6	*Frindle* by Andrew Clements
1999	4-6	*101 Ways to Bug Your Parents* by Lee Wardlaw
2000	4-6	*Harry Potter and the Sorcerer's Stone* by J. K. Rowling
2001	4-6	*Among the Hidden* by Margaret Peterson Haddix
2002	4-6	*Because of Winn-Dixie* by Kate DiCamillo
2003	4-6	*Love That Dog* by Sharon Creech

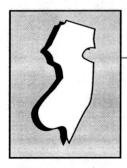

NEW JERSEY

Garden State Children's Book Award

1977 <www.njla.org/honorsawards/> 2-5 E
(Easy to Read), 2-5 S (Easy to Read Series), 2-5
(Fiction), 2-5 N (Nonfiction)

SPONSOR: Children's Services Section of the New Jersey Library
Association

PURPOSE: To recognize a combination of excellence and popular appeal
in books for younger readers. These books will encourage children in
grades two through five to keep reading, as well as stimulate and captivate
them through the printed word and quality illustrations.

NAME ORIGIN: Named after the state nickname—Garden State.

SELECTION CRITERIA: A committee selects up to 20 titles in each
category. The books must be original (no reprints, re-illustrations, or
retellings) and American hardcovers published three years before the award
year. The committee selections emphasize literary quality and artistic merit,
while keeping in mind popularity.

VOTING: Children may vote at their school or public libraries. They are
encouraged to read as many books as they can and do not have to vote in
all the categories.

1977	2-5	*Encyclopedia Brown Lends a Hand* by Donald Sobol
	2-5 E	*Dinosaur Time* by Peggy Parish
	2-5 N	*On the Track of Bigfoot* by Marion T. Place
1978	2-5	*Dorrie's Book* by Marilyn Sachs
	2-5 E	*Owl at Home* by Arnold Lobel
	2-5 N	*How Kittens Grow* by Millicent Selsam
1979	2-5	*Nobody Has to Be a Kid Forever* by Hila Colman
	2-5 E	*Hattie Rabbit* by Dick Gackenbach
	2-5 E	*Heather's Feathers* by Leatie Weiss
	2-5 N	*A Very Young Dancer* by Jill Krementz
1980	2-5	*Ramona and Her Father* by Beverly Cleary
	2-5 E	*Teach Us, Amelia Bedelia* by Peggy Parish
	2-5 N	*The Quicksand Book* by Tomie dePaola
1981	2-5	*The Great Gilly Hopkins* by Katherine Paterson
	2-5 E	*Grasshopper on the Road* by Arnold Lobel

	2-5 N	*Tyrannosaurus Rex* by Millicent Selsam
1982	2-5	*Ramona and Her Mother* by Beverly Cleary
	2-5 E	*Mrs. Gaddy and the Ghost* by Mary Q. Steele
	2-5 N	*Mummies Made in Egypt* by Aliki
1983	2-5	*Superfudge* by Judy Blume
	2-5 E	*Commander Toad in Space* by Jane Yolen
	2-5 E	*Clams Can't Sing* by James Stevenson
	2-5 N	*A Show of Hands: Say It in Sign Language* by Mary Beth Sullivan
1984	2-5	*Ramona Quimby, Age 8* by Beverly Cleary
	2-5 E	*Nate the Great and the Missing Key* by Marjorie Sharmat
	2-5 N	*A Light in the Attic* by Shel Silverstein
1985	2-5	*Ralph S. Mouse* by Beverly Cleary
	2-5 E	*Nate the Great and the Snowy Trail* by Majorie Sharmat
	2-5 N	*It's BASIC: The ABC's of Computer Programming* by Shelley Lipson
1986	2-5	*Dear Mr. Henshaw* by Beverly Cleary
	2-5 E	*M & M and the Bad News Babies* by Pat Ross
	2-5 N	*Draw 50 Monsters,Creeps, Superheroes, Demons, Dragons, Nerds, Dirts, Ghouls, Giants, Vampires, Zombies and Other Curiosa* by Lee J. Ames
1987	2-5	*Anastasia, Ask Your Analyst* by Lois Lowry
	2-5 E	*In a Dark, Dark Room: and Other Scary Stories* by Alvin Schwartz
	2-5 N	*The New Kid on the Block: Poems* by Jack Prelutsky
1988	2-5	*Sarah, Plain and Tall* by Patricia MacLachlan
	2-5 E	*Amelia Bedelia Goes Camping* by Peggy Parish
	2-5 N	*How They Built the Statue of Liberty* by Mary J. Shapiro
1989	2-5	*Anastasia Has the Answers* by Lois Lowry
	2-5 E	*Merry Christmas, Amelia Bedelia* by Peggy Parish
	2-5 N	*To Space and Back* by Sally Ride and Susan Oakie
1990	2-5	*Nighty-Nightmare* by James Howe
	2-5 E	*Henry and Mudge in Puddle Trouble* by Cynthia Rylant
	2-5 N	*Koko's Story* by Francine Patterson
1991	2-5	*The Burning Questions of Bingo Brown* by Betsy Byars
	2-5	*Teacher's Pet* by Johanna Horwitz
	2-5 E	*Fox on the Job* by James Marshall
	2-5 N	*Volcanoes* by Seymour Simon
1992	2-5	*Wayside School Is Falling Down* by Louis Sachar
	2-5 E	*Henry and Mudge Get the Cold Shivers* by Cynthia Rylant
	2-5 N	*The Magic School Bus Inside the Human Body* by Joanna Cole
1993	2-5	*Muggie Maggie* by Beverly Cleary
	2-5 E	*Henry and Mudge and the Happy Cat* by Cynthia Rylant

	2-5 N	*The Magic School Bus Lost in the Solar System* by Joanna Cole
1994	2-5	*School's Out* by Johanna Hurwitz
	2-5 E	*Henry and Mudge and the Bedtime Thumps* by Cynthia Rylant
	2-5 N	*Big Cats* by Seymour Simon
1995	2-5	*Attaboy, Sam!* by Lois Lowry
	2-5 E	*Henry and Mudge and the Long Weekend* by Cynthia Rylant
	2-5 N	*The Magic School Bus on the Ocean Floor* by Joanna Cole
1996	2-5	*Nibble, Nibble, Jenny Archer* by Ellen Conford
	2-5 E	*Henry and Mudge and the Wild Wind* by Cynthia Rylant
	2-5 N	*My Visit to the Aquarium* by Aliki
1997	2-5	*Amber Brown Is Not a Crayon* by Paula Danziger
	2-5 E	*Henry and Mudge and the Careful Cousin* by Cynthia Rylant
	2-5 N	*The Big Bug Book* by Margery Facklam
1998	2-5	*Wayside School Gets a Little Stranger* by Louis Sachar
	2-5 E	*Henry and Mudge and the Best Day of All* by Cynthia Rylant
	2-5 N	*The Magic School Bus Inside a Hurricane* by Joanna Cole
1999	2-5	*Forever Amber Brown* by Paula Danziger
	2-5 E	*Arthur's Reading Race* by Marc Brown
	2-5 N	*The Magic School Bus Inside a Beehive* by Joanna Cole
2000	2-5	*The Adventures of Captain Underpants: An Epic Novel* by Dav Pilkey
	2-5 E	*Henry and Mudge in the Family Trees* by Cynthia Rylant
	2-5 N	*Lou Gehrig: The Luckiest Man* by David Adler
2001	2-5	*Holes* by Louis Sachar
	2-5 E	*Bathtime for Biscuit* by Alyssa Satin Capucilli
	2-5 N	*Lives of the Presidents: Fame, Shame (And What the Neighbors Thought)* by Kathleen Krull
	2-5 S	*Henry and Mudge and the Sneaky Crackers* by Cynthia Rylant
2002	2-5	*Captain Underpants and the Attack of the Talking Toilets: Another Epic Novel* by Dav Pilkey
	2-5 E	*One Saturday Afternoon* by Barbara Baker
	2-5 N	*Behold . . . the Dragons!* by Gail Gibbons
	2-5 S	*Henry and Mudge and the Snowman Plan* by Cynthia Rylant
2003	2-5	*Judy Moody* by Megan McDonald
	2-5 E	*Tiny Goes to the Library* by Cari Meister
	2-5 N	*So You Want to Be President?* by Judith St. George
	2-5 S	*Henry and Mudge and Annie's Perfect Pet* by Cynthia Rylant
2004	2-5	*Captain Underpants and the Wrath of the Wicked Wedgie Woman* by Dav Pilkey
	2-5 E	*It's Justin Time, Amber Brown* by Paula Danziger

2-5 N *The Dinosaurs of Waterhouse Hawkins: An Illuminating History of Mr. Waterhouse Hawkins, Artist and Lecturer* by Barbara Kerley

2-5 S *Nate the Great, San Francisco Detective* by Marjorie and Mitchell Sharmat

NEW JERSEY

Garden State Teen Book Award
1995   <www.njla.org/honorsawards/book/teen.html>
6-8, 9-12, 6-12 N (Nonfiction)

SPONSOR: Adult/Young Adult Section of the New Jersey Library Association

PURPOSE: To make New Jersey students in grades six through twelve aware of appealing, quality, award-winning books and to promote reading and literacy.

NAME ORIGIN: Named after the state nickname—Garden State.

SELECTION CRITERIA: The award's committee, representing libraries from throughout the state, selects the nominees based on teen appeal and quality of writing from the previous year's "Best Books" lists. The lists used are: *Best Books for Young Adults, Quick Picks*, the Alex Awards, the Printz and Newbery winners, and *School Library Journal, Booklist* and *VOYA* best of the best lists.

VOTING: Students may read and vote for as few or as many books as they would like. Students may vote on any of the lists.

1995	6-8	*Nothing But the Truth: A Documentary Novel* by Avi
	9-12	*Children of the Night* by Dan Simmons
	6-12 N	*Into the Mummy's Tomb: The Real-Life Discovery of Tuthankhamen's Treasures* by Nicholas Reeves
1996	6-8	*The Giver* by Lois Lowry
	9-12	*Thor* by Wayne Smith
	6-12 N	*Anne Frank, Beyond the Diary: A Photographic Remembrance* by Ruud van der Rol
1997	6-8	*Loch: A Novel* by Paul Zindel
	9-12	*Driver's Ed* by Caroline Cooney
	6-12 N	*Kids at Work: Louis Hines and the Crusade Against Child Labor* by Russell Freedman
1998	6-8	*Slot Machine* by Chris Lynch
	9-12	*Relic* by Douglas Preston and Lincoln Child
	6-12 N	*The Hot Zone* by Richard Preston

1999	6-8	*Brian's Winter* by Gary Paulsen
	9-12	*Mount Dragon* by Douglas Preston and Lincoln Child
	6-12 N	*Into the Wild* by Jon Krakauer
2000	6-8	*Tangerine* by Edward Bloor
	9-12	*Blood and Chocolate* by Annette Curtis Klause
	6-12 N	*Into Thin Air: A Personal Account of the Mount Everest Disaster* by Jon Krakauer
2001	6-8	*Life in the Fat Lane* by Cherie Bennett
	9-12	*The Killer's Cousin* by Nancy Werlin
	6-12 N	*How Rude! The Teenage Guide to Good Manners, Proper Behavior and Not Grossing People Out* by Alex Packer
2002	6-8	*Skellig* by David Almond
	9-12	*Speak* by Laurie Halse Anderson
	6-12 N	*Spiders in the Hairdo: Modern Urban Legends* by David Holt and Bill Mooney
2003	6-8	*Stargirl* by Jerry Spinelli
	9-12	*Angus, Thongs and Full Frontal Snogging: Confessions of Georgia Nicolson* by Louise Rennison
	6-12 N	*The Worst-Case Scenario Survival Handbook* by Joshua Piven

New Mexico

Land of Enchantment Book Award
1981   <www.loebookaward.com>   3-6
(Children's), 6-9 (Young Adult)

SPONSOR: New Mexico Library Association, New Mexico Council of the International Reading Association, New Mexico State Library

PURPOSE: To encourage the youth of New Mexico to read outstanding books of literary quality.

NAME ORIGIN: Named after the state nickname—Land of Enchantment.

SELECTION CRITERIA: Books on the list are chosen by a committee from the New Mexico Library Association and the New Mexico Council of the International Reading Association working with children and young adults who read and discuss annually more than 100 titles. Criteria for selection of the lists include: books written by an author living in the United States; copyright within five years prior to award date; literary quality and favorable reviews; interest, appeal, and developmental levels for students in grades three through nine.

VOTING: Any New Mexico child, provided they have read or heard at least three books from the list appropriate to them, is eligible to vote.

1981	4-8	*Ramona and Her Father* by Beverly Cleary
1982	4-8	*Bunnicula: A Rabbit Tale of Mystery* by James Howe
1983	4-8	*Summer of Fear* by Lois Duncan
1984	4-8	*Superfudge* by Judy Blume
1985	4-8	*Nothing's Fair in Fifth Grade* by Barthe DeClements
1986	4-8	*Thirteen Ways to Sink a Sub* by Jamie Gilson
1987	4-8	*Zucchini* by Barbara Dana
1988	4-8	*The Dollhouse Murders* by Betty Ren Wright
1989	4-8	*Sixth Grade Can Really Kill You* by Barthe DeClements
1990	4-8	*There's a Boy in the Girls' Bathroom* by Louis Sachar
1991	4-8	*Pecos Bill: A Tall Tale* by Steven Kellogg
1992	4-8	*Wayside School Is Falling Down* by Louis Sachar
1993	4-8	*Maniac Magee* by Jerry Spinelli
1994	4-8	*Shiloh* by Phyllis Reynolds Naylor
1995	4-8	*Terror at the Zoo* by Peg Kehret

1996	4-8	*Knights of the Kitchen Table* by Jon Scieszka
1997	4-8	*The Giver* by Lois Lowry
1998	4-8	*The Best School Year Ever* by Barbara Robinson
1999	4-8	*Poppy* by Avi
2000	3-6	*Library Lil* by Suzanne Williams
	6-9	*The Watson's Go to Birmingham—1963* by Christopher Paul Curtis
2001	3-6	*A Spoon for Every Bite* by Joe Hayes
	6-9	*Holes* by Louis Sachar
2002	3-6	*Rumpelstiltskin's Daughter* by Diane Stanley
	6-9	*Ghost Canoe* by Will Hobbs
2003	3-6	*Because of Winn-Dixie* by Kate DiCamillo
	6-9	*Bud, Not Buddy* by Christopher Paul Curtis

NEW YORK

Charlotte Award
1990 <www.nysreading.org/awards/charlotte/
index.htm> K-3 (Primary), 3-6 (Intermediate),
6-12 (Young Adult)

SPONSOR: New York Reading Association

PURPOSE: To encourage students to read outstanding literature and
ultimately become lifelong readers. Additionally, the award recognizes the
authors and illustrators of such literature.

NAME ORIGIN: Named for the main character in E. B. White's
Charlotte's Web.

SELECTION CRITERIA: The list is published in odd-numbered years,
and the award is given in even-numbered years.

VOTING: Students may have read or heard the books to become qualified
voters. Students are encouraged to read all titles in a category, but it is not a
requirement. Students may read books in more than one category and are
entitled to one vote in each category for which they qualify.

1990	K-3	*The Magic School Bus at the Waterworks* by Joanna Cole. Bruce Degan, ill.
	3-5	*Piggins* by Jane Yolen
	6-8	*The Way Things Work* by David Macauley
1992	K-3	*The Great Kapok Tree: A Tale of the Amazon Rain Forest* by Lynne Cherry
	3-5	*Number the Stars* by Lois Lowry
	6-8	*Maniac Magee* by Jerry Spinelli
	6-12	*Fallen Angels* by Walter Dean Myers
1994	K-3	*Rescue Josh McGuire* by Ben Mikaelsen
	3-5	*The Rag Coat* by Lauren Mills
	6-8	*There's a Girl in My Hammerlock* by Jerry Spinelli
	6-12	*Nothing But the Truth: A Documentary Novel* by Avi
1996	K-3	*Owl Babies* by Martin Waddell. Patrick Benson, ill.
	3-5	*First Apple* by Ching Yeung Russell
	6-8	*Tell Them We Remember: The Story of the Holocaust* by Susan D. Bachrach

	6-12	*Phoenix Rising* by Karen Hesse
1998	K-3	*When I Was Five* by Arthur Howard
	3-6	*Mick Harte Was Here* by Barbara Park
	6-12	*Freak the Mighty* by Rodman Philbrick
2000	K-3	*Rotten Teeth* by Laura Simms. David Catrow, ill.
	3-6	*I Was a Third Grade Science Project* by Mary Jane Auch
	6-12	*Harry Potter and the Sorcerer's Stone* by J. K. Rowling
2002	K-3	*Click, Clack, Moo: Cows That Type* by Doreen Cronin. Betsy Lewin, ill.
	3-6	*Because of Winn-Dixie* by Kate DiCamillo
	6-12	*Give a Boy a Gun* by Todd Strasser

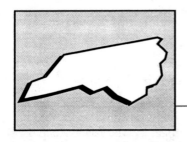

NORTH CAROLINA

North Carolina Children's Book Award
1992   <www.bookhive.org/nccba>   K-3 (Picture Book), 4-6 (Junior Book)

SPONSOR: North Carolina School Library Media Association, Children's Services and North Carolina Association of School Librarians sections of the North Carolina Library Association

PURPOSE: To broaden students' awareness of current literature, to promote reading aloud with students in the early grades as a means of introducing reading as a pleasure, and to give recognition and honor to children's favorite books and authors.

SELECTION CRITERIA: Students nominate books that have been published within the last three years. The list is checked for balance among genres. North Carolina authors and illustrators or North Carolina settings gain extra consideration, but are not necessarily added to the final list. The picture book list contains 15 to 25 titles and the junior book list contains 10 to 20 titles.

VOTING: Students must read five picture books and three junior books from the list in order to vote.

1992	K-3	*In a Dark, Dark Room: and Other Scary Stories* by Alvin Schwartz. Dirk Zimmer, ill.
1993	K-3	*The Seven Chinese Brothers* by Margaret Mahy. Jean Tseng and Mou-Sien Tseng, ill.
1994	K-3	*The Stinky Cheese Man and Other Fairly Stupid Tales* by Jon Scieszka. Lane Smith, ill.
1995	K-3	*The Rainbow Fish* by Marcus Pfister
	4-6	*The Boys Start the War* by Phyllis Reynolds Naylor
1996	K-3	*The Man Who Tricked a Ghost* by Laurence Yep. Isadore Seltzer, ill.
	4-6	*My Teacher Fried My Brains* by Bruce Coville
1997	K-3	*Officer Buckle and Gloria* by Peggy Rathman
	4-6	*Wicked Jack* by Connie Wooldridge
1998	K-3	*Roses Are Pink, Your Feet Really Stink* by Diane DeGroat

	4-6	*Shiloh Season* by Phyllis Reynolds Naylor
1999	K-3	*Verdi* by Janell Cannon
	4-6	*Frindle* by Andrew Clements
2000	K-3	*The Ghost of Sifty-Sifty Sam* by Angela Shelf Medearis. Jacqueline Rogers, ill.
	4-6	*Crash* by Jerry Spinelli
2001	K-3	*Hooway for Wodney Wat!* by Helen Lester. Lynn Munsinger, ill.
	4-6	*Tornado* by Betsy Byars
2002	K-3	*A Bad Case of Stripes* by David Shannon
	4-6	*Salt in His Shoes: Michael Jordan in Pursuit of a Dream* by Deloris Jordan and Roslyn M. Jordan
2003	K-3	*More Parts* by Tedd Arnold
	4-6	*Fearless Jack* by Paul Brett Johnson

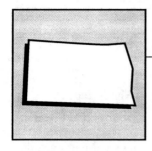

NORTH DAKOTA

Flickertail Children's Book Award

1978   <http://ndsl.lib.state.nd.us/ndla/ftaward.htm>
PreK-3 (Picture Book), 3-8 (Juvenile Book)

SPONSOR: North Dakota Library Association, School Library and Youth Services Section

PURPOSE: To encourage children to read good literature.

NAME ORIGIN: Named after the state mammal—Flickertail.

SELECTION CRITERIA: The book must have been published in the last five years and must be popular within the library nominating it. Once a title has won, it cannot be nominated again. Each list contains five titles.

VOTING: Children must read or hear at least three books in order to vote in the Picture Book category, and at least two books from the Juvenile Book category.

1978	3-8	*Star Wars* by George Lucas
1979	3-8	*Are You There, God? It's Me, Margaret* by Judy Blume
1980	3-8	*Tales of a Fourth Grade Nothing* by Judy Blume
1981	PreK-3	*Curious George* by H. A. Rey
	3-8	*Where the Red Fern Grows: The Story of Two Dogs and a Boy* by Wilson Rawls
1982	PreK-3	*The Fox and the Hound* by Walt Disney Productions
	3-8	*Superfudge* by Judy Blume
1983	PreK-3	*E. T. Extra-Terrestrial Storybook* by William Kotzwinkle. Melissa Mathison, ill.
	3-8	*Blubber* by Judy Blume
1984	PreK-3	*A Sister for Sam* by Evelyn Mason
	3-8	*Return of the Jedi: The Storybook Based on the Movie* by Joan Vinge
1985	PreK-3	*Charlie and the Chocolate Factory* by Roald Dahl
	3-8	*Charlie and the Chocolate Factory* by Roald Dahl
1986		No Award Given
1987	PreK-3	*The Day Jimmy's Boa Ate the Wash* by Trinka Hakes Noble. Steven Kellogg, ill.
	3-8	*Superfudge* by Judy Blume

1988	PreK-3	*Miss Nelson Has a Field Day* by Harry Allard. James Marshall, ill.
	3-8	*Nothing's Fair in Fifth Grade* by Barthe DeClements
1989	PreK-3	*Love You Forever* by Robert Munsch. Sheila McGraw, ill.
	3-8	*On My Honor* by Marion Dane Bauer
1990	PreK-3	*Meanwhile, Back at the Ranch* by Trinka Hakes Noble
	3-8	*Hatchet* by Gary Paulsen
1991	PreK-3	*No Jumping on the Bed!* by Tedd Arnold
	3-8	*How to Fight a Girl* by Thomas Rockwell
1992	PreK-3	*Scared Silly: A Halloween Treat* by James Howe
	3-8	*Maniac Magee* by Jerry Spinelli
1993	PreK-3	*The Signmaker's Assistant* by Tedd Arnold
	3-8	*Fudge-A-Mania* by Judy Blume
1994	PreK-3	*The Stinky Cheese Man and Other Fairly Stupid Tales* by Jon Scieszka. Lane Smith, ill.
	3-8	*Shiloh* by Phyllis Reynolds Naylor
1995	PreK-3	*Easter Egg Farm* by Mary Jane Auch
	3-8	*The River* by Gary Paulsen
1996	PreK-3	*My Rotten Redheaded Older Brother* by Patricia Polacco
	3-8	*The Best School Year Ever* by Barbara Robinson
1997	PreK-3	*The Library Dragon* by Carmen Agra Deedy. Michael P. White, ill.
	3-8	*Mick Harte Was Here* by Barbara Park
1998	PreK-3	*Casey in the Bath* by Cynthia DeFelice. Chris Demarest, ill.
	3-8	*Rescue Josh McGuire* by Ben Mikaelsen
1999	PreK-3	*Grandpa's Teeth* by Rod Clement
	3-8	*Shiloh Season* by Phyllis Reynolds Naylor
2000	PreK-3	*No, David!* by David Shannon
	3-8	*Holes* by Louis Sachar
2001	PreK-3	*Hooway for Wodney Wat!* by Helen Lester. Lynn Munsinger, ill.
	3-8	*Frindle* by Andrew Clements
2002	PreK-3	*Bark, George* by Jules Feiffer
	3-8	*Touching Spirit Bear* by Ben Mikaelsen
2003	PreK-3	*Armadillo Tattletale* by Helen Ketteman. Keith Graves, ill.
	3-8	*Skeleton Man* by Joseph Bruchac

OHIO

Buckeye Children's Book Award

1982   <www.bcbookaward.info/>   K-2, 3-5, 6-8

SPONSOR: Ohio Council International Reading Association, Ohio Educational Library Media Association, Ohio Council of Teachers of English and Language Arts, Ohio Library Council, State Library of Ohio

PURPOSE: To encourage children in Ohio to read literature critically; to promote teacher and librarian involvement in children's literature programs; and to commend authors of such literature.

NAME ORIGIN: Named after the state nickname—Buckeye State.

SELECTION CRITERIA: The book must have been written by an author who is a citizen of the United States; be originally copyrighted in the U.S. within the last three years preceding the nomination and be first published in book form (movie spin-offs are not eligible for nomination). Previous winning book titles are not eligible for nomination. Only Ohio children can nominate books. There is no teacher-librarian prepared list of books from which to read. Books are nominated one year and voted on the next.

1982	K-2	*The Berenstain Bears and the Spooky Old Tree* by Stan and Jan Berenstain
	4-8	*Superfudge* by Judy Blume
1983	K-2	*Grandpa's Ghost Stories* by James Flora
	4-8	*Tiger Eyes* by Judy Blume
1984	K-2	*E. T. Extra-Terrestrial Storybook* by William Kotzwinkle. Melissa Mathison, ill.
	4-8	*Nothing's Fair in Fifth Grade* by Barthe DeClements
1985	K-2	*The Berenstain Bears Get in a Fight* by Stan and Jan Berenstain
	3-5	*Ramona Quimby, Age 8* by Beverly Cleary
	6-8	*A Light in the Attic* by Shel Silverstein
1987	K-2	*In a Dark, Dark Room: and Other Scary Stories* by Alvin Schwartz. Dirk Zimmer, ill.
	3-5	*Scary Stories to Tell in the Dark* by Alvin Schwartz
	6-8	*Thirteen Ways to Sink a Sub* by Jamie Gilson
1989	K-2	*If You Give a Mouse a Cookie* by Laura Numeroff. Felicia Bond, ill.

	3-5	*More Scary Stories to Tell in the Dark* by Alvin Schwartz
	6-8	*Sixth Grade Can Really Kill You* by Barthe DeClements
1991	K-2	*Polar Express* by Chris Van Allsburg
	3-5	*There's a Boy in the Girls' Bathroom* by Louis Sachar
	6-8	*Hatchet* by Gary Paulsen
1993	K-2	*The Very Quiet Cricket* by Eric Carle
	3-5	*Scary Stories 3: More Tales to Chill Your Bones* by Alvin Schwartz
	6-8	*Maniac Magee* by Jerry Spinelli
1995	K-2	*The Stinky Cheese Man and Other Fairly Stupid Tales* by Jon Scieszka. Lane Smith, ill.
	3-5	*Shiloh* by Phyllis Reynolds Naylor
	6-8	*Say Cheese and Die* by R. L. Stine
1997	K-2	*Dogzilla: Starring Flash, Rabies, Dwayne, and Introducing Leia as the Monster* by Dav Pilkey
	3-5	*The Haunted Mask II* by R. L. Stine
	6-8	*The Giver* by Lois Lowry
1999	K-2	*Verdi* by Janell Cannon
	3-5	*Wayside School Gets a Little Stranger* by Louis Sachar
	6-8	*Seedfolks* by Paul Fleischman
2001	K-2	*Bark, George* by Jules Feiffer
	3-5	*The Adventures of Captain Underpants: An Epic Novel* by Dav Pilkey
	6-8	*Holes* by Louis Sachar
2003	K-2	*David Goes to School* by David Shannon
	3-5	*Captain Underpants and the Wrath of the Wicked Wedgie Woman* by Dav Pilkey
	6-8	*Chicken Soup for the Preteen Soul: 101 Stories of Changes, Choices and Growing Up for Kids*

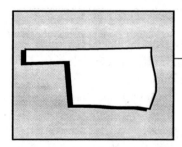

OKLAHOMA

Sequoyah Book Awards

1959   <www.sequoyahbookaward.com>
3-6 (Children's Book), 6-9 (Young Adult)

SPONSOR: Oklahoma Library Association

PURPOSE: To encourage the students of Oklahoma to read books of literary quality.

NAME ORIGIN: With this award, Oklahoma honors the Native American leader Sequoyah, for his unique achievement in creating the Cherokee syllabary. Sequoyah chose 85 symbols to represent all spoken sounds of the Cherokee language. In so doing, he created a way to preserve his people's language and culture.

SELECTION CRITERIA: Books must have originality, literary quality, interest, appeal, and be developmentally appropriate for the designated age level. The title must be published three years before the award date, and the author must be living in the United States.

VOTING: Students must read a minimum of three titles from the list to be eligible to vote.

1959	3-6	*Old Yeller* by Fred Gipson
1960	3-6	*Black Gold* by Marguerite Henry
1961	3-6	*Have Space Suit—Will Travel* by Robert A. Heinlein
1962	3-6	*The Helen Keller Story* by Catherine O. Peare
1963	3-6	*Mystery of the Haunted Pool* by Phyllis A. Whitney
1964	3-6	*Where the Panther Screams* by William Robinson
1965	3-6	*A Wrinkle in Time* by Madeleine L'Engle
1966	3-6	*Rascal* by Sterling North
1967	3-6	*Harriet the Spy* by Louise Fitzhugh
1968	3-6	*Gentle Ben* by Walt Morey
1969	3-6	*Blackbeard's Ghost* by Ben Stahl
1970	3-6	*Mustang: Wild Spirit of the West* by Marguerite Henry
1971	3-6	*Ramona the Pest* by Beverly Cleary
1972	3-6	*The Man in the Box: A Story from Vietnam* by Marylois Dunn
1973	3-6	*The Trumpet of the Swan* by E. B. White
1974	3-6	*Flight of the White Wolf* by Mel Ellis

1975	3-6	*Tales of a Fourth Grade Nothing* by Judy Blume
1976	3-6	*How to Eat Fried Worms* by Thomas Rockwell
1977	3-6	*The Toothpaste Millionaire* by Jean Merrill
1978	3-6	*Shoeshine Girl* by Clyde Robert Bulla
1979	3-6	*Summer of the Monkeys* by Wilson Rawls
1980	3-6	*Kid Power* by Susan Beth Pfeffer
1981	3-6	*Get-Away Car* by Eleanor Lowenton Clymer
1982	3-6	*Bunnicula: A Rabbit Tale of Mystery* by James Howe
1983	3-6	*A Dog Called Kitty* by Bill Wallace
1984	3-6	*The Cybil War* by Betsy Byars
1985	3-6	*Thirteen Ways to Sink a Sub* by Jamie Gilson
1986	3-6	*Dear Mr. Henshaw* by Beverly Cleary
1986	3-6	*Just Tell Me When We're Dead!* by Ellen Conford
1987	3-6	*Night of the Twisters* by Ivy Ruckman
1988	3-6	*Christina's Ghost* by Betty Ren Wright
	6-9	*Abby, My Love* by Hadley Irwin
1989	3-6	*The Sixth Grade Sleepover* by Eve Bunting
	6-9	*The Other Side of Dark* by Joan Lowery Nixon
1990	3-6	*Fudge* by Charlotte Graeber
	6-9	*Hatchet* by Gary Paulsen
1991	3-6	*Beauty* by Bill Wallace
	6-9	*A Sudden Silence* by Eve Bunting
1992	3-6	*The Doll in the Garden: A Ghost Story* by Mary Downing Hahn
	6-9	*Appointment With a Stranger* by Jean Thesman
1993	3-6	*Weasel* by Cynthia DeFelice
	6-9	*The Silver Kiss* by Annette Curtis Klause
1994	3-6	*Shiloh* by Phyllis Reynolds Naylor
	6-9	*What Daddy Did: A Novel* by Neal Shusterman
1995	3-6	*Horror at the Haunted House* by Peg Kehret
	6-9	*Flight #116 Is Down* by Caroline Cooney
1996	3-6	*The Ghosts of Mercy Manor* by Betty Ren Wright
	6-9	*The Giver* by Lois Lowry
1997	3-6	*Nasty, Stinky Sneakers* by Eve Bunting
	6-9	*Walk Two Moons* by Sharon Creech
1998	3-6	*Titanic Crossing* by Barbara Williams
	6-9	*Running Out of Time* by Margaret Peterson Haddix
1999	3-6	*101 Ways to Bug Your Parents* by Lee Wardlaw
	6-9	*Danger Zone* by David Klass
2000	3-6	*The Million Dollar Shot* by Dan Gutman
	6-9	*I Have Lived a Thousand Years: Growing Up in the Holocaust* by Livia Bitton-Jackson
2001	3-6	*Holes* by Louis Sachar
	6-9	*Holes* by Louis Sachar

2002	3-6	*Dork in Disguise* by Carol Gorman
	6-9	*Speak* by Laurie Halse Anderson
2003	3-6	*Because of Winn-Dixie* by Kate DiCamillo
	6-9	*Define Normal* by Julie Anne Peters
2004	3-6	*Skeleton Man* by Joseph Bruchac
	6-9	*Sisterhood of the Traveling Pants* by Ann Brashares

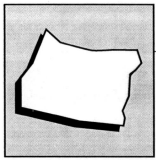

OREGON

Beverly Cleary Children's Choice Award

2003 <www.oema.net/cleary/index.htm> 2-3

SPONSOR: Oregon Educational Media Association

PURPOSE: To encourage reading by highlighting good quality literature (fiction and nonfiction) written on the second through third grade reading level, taking into account text, format, and the illustrations of the books. This award will encourage books that students may not otherwise find on their own and are not necessarily the popular best sellers.

NAME ORIGIN: The award is named for Oregon native Beverly Cleary, librarian and author of many children's books.

SELECTION CRITERIA: The books for the list should be quality literature—fiction or nonfiction—published within three years, at a third-grade reading level (taking into account vocabulary, graphic support, physical layout of the books).

VOTING: Students must read or hear two of the nominated titles to be eligible to vote.

2003   2-3 *Judy Moody* by Megan McDonald

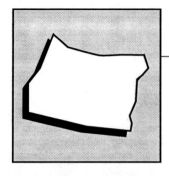

OREGON

Patricia Gallagher Picture Book Award

1998   <www.oregonread.org/gallagheraward.html>   K-3

SPONSOR: Oregon Reading Association

PURPOSE: To promote literacy and a love of reading.

NAME ORIGIN: Named for Patricia Gallagher, a retired Western Oregon professor of children's literature and a former president of the Oregon Reading Association.

SELECTION CRITERIA: The books must be available in paperback, be published within four years, hold an innate appeal to children, and have quality text and illustrations. The list contains five books.

VOTING: Oregon school-age children vote.

1998	K-3	*Mrs. Merriwether's Musical Cat* by Carol Purdy. Petra Mathers, ill.
1999	K-3	*The Rough-Face Girl* by Rafe Martin. David Shannon, ill.
2000	K-3	*The Dragon Prince: A Chinese Beauty and the Beast Tale* by Laurence Yep. Kam Mak, ill.
2001	K-3	*Heat Wave* by Helen Ketteman. Scott Goto, ill.
2002	K-3	*The Lost and Found* by Mark Teague
2003	K-3	*Small Brown Dog's Bad Remembering Day* by Mike Gibbie. Barbara Nascimbeni, ill.

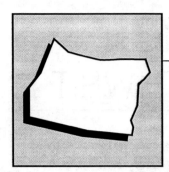

OREGON

See Pacific Northwest

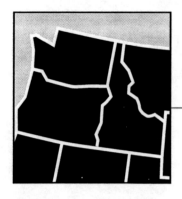

PACIFIC NORTHWEST

Young Reader's Choice Award

1940   <http://pnla.org/yrca/index.htm>   4-6
(Junior), 7-9 (Intermediate), 10-12 (Senior)

SPONSOR: Pacific Northwest Library Association (Washington, Oregon, Alaska, Idaho, Montana, British Columbia and Alberta)

PURPOSE: To encourage young readers; to promote reading for pleasure; and the lifelong love of reading and learning.

SELECTION CRITERIA: The principle criterion considered in placing a title on the list is the number of nominations received. Other considerations include reading enjoyment; reading and interest level; genre and gender representation; racial diversity; diversity of social, political, economic, or religious viewpoints; effectiveness of expression; creativity; imagination; availability in the United States and Canada; and availability in paperback. All books must have an original American or Canadian copyright date three years prior to when it will appear on the list.

VOTING: Students must read three or more titles and may cast only one vote per ballot.

1940	4-8	*Paul Bunyan Swings His Axe* by Dell J. McCormick
1941	4-8	*Mr. Popper's Penguins* by Richard and Florence Atwater
1942	4-8	*By the Shores of Silver Lake* by Laura Ingalls Wilder
1943	4-8	*Lassie Come Home* by Eric Knight
1944	4-8	*The Black Stallion* by Walter Farley
1945	4-8	*Snow Treasure* by Marie McSwigan
1946	4-8	*The Return of Silver Chief* by Jack O'Brien
1947	4-8	*Homer Price* by Robert McCloskey
1948	4-8	*The Black Stallion Returns* by Walter Farley
1949	4-8	*Cowboy Boots* by Shannon Garst
1950	4-8	*McElligot's Pool* by Dr. Seuss
1951	4-8	*King of the Wind* by Marguerite Henry
1952	4-8	*Sea Star* by Marguerite Henry
1953	4-8	No Award Given
1954	4-8	No Award Given

1955	4-8	No Award Given
1956	4-8	*Miss Pickerell Goes to Mars* by Ellen MacGregor
1957	4-8	*Henry and Ribsy* by Beverly Cleary
1958	4-8	*Golden Mare* by William Corbin
1959	4-8	*Old Yeller* by Fred Gipson
1960	4-8	*Henry and the Paper Route* by Beverly Cleary
1961	4-8	*Danny Dunn and the Homework Machine* by Jay Williams
1962	4-8	*The Swamp Fox of the Revolution* by Stewart Holbrook
1963	4-8	*Danny Dunn on the Ocean Floor* by Jay Williams
1964	4-8	*The Incredible Journey* by Sheila Burnford
1965	4-8	*John F. Kennedy and PT-109* by Richard Tregaskis
1966	4-8	*Rascal* by Sterling North
1967	4-8	*Chitty Chitty Bang Bang* by Ian Fleming
1968	4-8	*The Mouse and the Motorcycle* by Beverly Cleary
1969	4-8	*Henry Reed's Baby-sitting Service* by Keith Robertson
1970	4-8	*Smoke* by William Corbin
1971	4-8	*Ramona the Pest* by Beverly Cleary
1972	4-8	*Encyclopedia Brown Keeps the Peace* by Donald Sobol
1973	4-8	No Award Given
1974	4-8	*Mrs. Frisby and the Rats of NIMH* by Robert O'Brien
1975	4-8	*Tales of a Fourth Grade Nothing* by Judy Blume
1976	4-8	*The Great Brain Reforms* by John D. Fitzgerald
1977	4-8	*Blubber* by Judy Blume
1978	4-8	*The Great Brain Does It Again* by John D. Fitzgerald
1979	4-8	*Roll of Thunder, Hear My Cry* by Mildred D. Taylor
1980	4-8	*Ramona and Her Father* by Beverly Cleary
1981	4-8	*Hail, Hail, Camp Timberwood* by Ellen Conford
1982	4-8	*Bunnicula: A Rabbit Tale of Mystery* by James Howe
1983	4-8	*Superfudge* by Judy Blume
1984	4-8	*The Indian in the Cupboard* by Lynne Reid Banks
1985	4-8	*Thirteen Ways to Sink a Sub* by Jamie Gilson
1986	4-8	*The Dollhouse Murders* by Betty Ren Wright
1987	4-8	*The War With Grandpa* by Robert Kimmel Smith
1988	4-8	*Sixth Grade Can Really Kill You* by Barthe DeClements
1989	4-8	*Wait Till Helen Comes* by Mary Downing Hahn
1990	4-8	*There's a Boy in the Girls' Bathroom* by Louis Sachar
1991	4-8	*Ten Kids, No Pets* by Ann M. Martin
	9-12	*Sex Education: A Novel* by Jenny Davis
1992	4-8	*Danger in Quicksand Swamp* by Bill Wallace
	9-12	*Eva* by Peter Dickinson
1993	4-8	*Maniac Magee* by Jerry Spinelli
	9-12	*The Face on the Milk Carton* by Caroline Cooney

1994	4-8	*Shiloh* by Phyllis Reynolds Naylor
	9-12	*Wolf By the Ears* by Ann Rinaldi
1995	4-8	*Terror at the Zoo* by Peg Kehret
	9-12	*Who Killed My Daughter? A True Story of a Mother's Search for Her Daughter's Murderer* by Lois Duncan
1996	4-8	*The Boys Start the War* by Phyllis Reynolds Naylor
	9-12	*The Giver* by Lois Lowry
1997	4-8	*Nasty, Stinky Sneakers* by Eve Bunting
	9-12	*Driver's Ed* by Caroline Cooney
1998	4-8	*Wayside School Gets a Little Stranger* by Louis Sachar
	9-12	*The Midwife's Apprentice* by Karen Cushman
1999	4-8	*Frindle* by Andrew Clements
	9-12	*SOS Titanic* by Eve Bunting
2000	4-8	*A Mouse Called Wolf* by Dick King-Smith
	9-12	*The Taking of Room 114* by Mel Glenn
2001	4-8	*Holes* by Louis Sachar
	9-12	*The Boxes* by William Sleator
2002	4-6	*Bud, Not Buddy* by Christopher Paul Curtis
	7-9	*Mary, Bloody Mary* by Carolyn Meyer
	10-12	*Rewind* by William Sleator
2003	4-6	*Because of Winn-Dixie* by Kate DiCamillo
	7-9	*No More Dead Dogs* by Gordon Korman
	10-12	*Hope Was Here* by Joan Bauer

PENNSYLVANIA

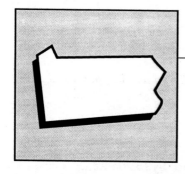

Pennsylvania Young Reader's Choice Award

1992 <www.psla.org/grantsandawards/
grantsandawards.php3> K-3, 3-6, 6-8

SPONSOR: Pennsylvania School Librarians Association

PURPOSE: To promote reading of quality books by young people in the Commonwealth of Pennsylvania; to promote teacher and librarian involvement in children's literature; to honor authors whose work has been recognized by the children of Pennsylvania.

SELECTION CRITERIA: Each book must have a copyright date within five years of the award's presentation; must be written by an author currently living in North America; must be appropriate to the reading/interest level of students in kindergarten through grade eight; must be of recognized literary quality; and may be fiction or nonfiction.

VOTING: Students must read or hear at least three books from the list in order to vote.

1992	3-5	*My Teacher Is an Alien* by Bruce Coville
	6-8	*Maniac Magee* by Jerry Spinelli
1993	3-5	*Fudge-A-Mania* by Judy Blume
	6-8	*Shiloh* by Phyllis Reynolds Naylor
1994	3-8	*The Stinky Cheese Man and Other Fairly Stupid Tales* by Jon Scieszka
1995	K-3	*Martha Speaks* by Susan Meddaugh
	3-8	*The Giver* by Lois Lowry
1996	K-3	*The Three Little Wolves and the Big Bad Pig* by Eugene Trivizas. Helen Oxenbury, ill.
	3-8	*The Sweetest Fig* by Chris Van Allsburg
1997	K-3	*Officer Buckle and Gloria* by Peggy Rathman
	3-6	*Swamp Angel* by Anne Isaacs
	6-8	*Heart of a Champion* by Carl Deuker
1998	K-3	*Buz* by Richard Egielski
	3-6	*The Best School Year Ever* by Barbara Robinson
	6-8	*Spying on Miss Muller* by Eve Bunting
1999	K-3	*No More Water in the Tub!* by Tedd Arnold

	3-6	*Shiloh Season* by Phyllis Reynolds Naylor
	6-8	*Crash* by Jerry Spinelli
2000	K-3	*The Adventures of Captain Underpants: An Epic Novel* by Dav Pilkey
	3-6	*Frindle* by Andrew Clements
	6-8	*Holes* by Louis Sachar
2001	K-3	*No, David!* by David Shannon
	3-6	*The Scrambled States of America* by Laurie Keller
	6-8	*Bud, Not Buddy* by Christopher Paul Curtis
2002	K-3	*A Bad Case of Stripes* by David Shannon
	3-6	*So You Want to Be President?* by Judith St. George
	6-8	*Among the Hidden* by Margaret Peterson Haddix
2003	K-3	*Humpty Dumpty Egg-splodes* by Kevin O'Malley
	3-6	*The Butterfly* by Patricia Polacco
	6-8	*The Two Princesses of Bamarre* by Gail Carson Levine

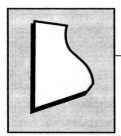

RHODE ISLAND

Rhode Island Children's Book Award
1991   <www.riema.org> Select "book links"   3-6

SPONSOR: A joint project of the Rhode Island State Council of the International Reading Association, the Rhode Island Library Association, and the Rhode Island Educational Media Association, coordinated by the Rhode Island Office of Library and Information Services.

PURPOSE: To encourage reading and enthusiasm for books.

SELECTION CRITERIA: Titles nominated should be appropriate for grades three through six; should have literary value; be published three years prior to the award; and must be in print. A title listed once may not be nominated again. Only one title per author may be nominated each year; authors must be currently living in the United States at the time of nomination; and the winning author will be excluded from nomination the following year. Editors of collected works by other authors are not considered. A committee of nine librarians, library media specialists, and teachers selects a list of 20 titles.

VOTING: Children who have read or heard three of the books from the list are eligible to vote at their school or public library.

1991	3-6	*Something Upstairs: A Tale of Ghosts* by Avi
1992	3-6	*Maniac Magee* by Jerry Spinelli
1993	3-6	*The Houdini Box* by Brian Selznick
1994	3-6	*The Stinky Cheese Man and Other Fairly Stupid Tales* by Jon Scieszka
1995	3-6	*The Sweetest Fig* by Chris Van Allsburg
1996	3-6	*Jacob and the Stranger* by Sally Derby
1997	3-6	*Mick Harte Was Here* by Barbara Park
1998	3-6	*Frindle* by Andrew Clements
1999	3-6	*The Adventures of Captain Underpants: An Epic Novel* by Dav Pilkey
2000	3-6	*Thank You, Mr. Falker* by Patricia Polacco
2001	3-6	*Weslandia* by Paul Fleischman
2002	3-6	*The Babe and I* by David Adler
2003	3-6	*Skeleton Man* by Joseph Bruchac

RHODE ISLAND

Rhode Island Teen Book Award
2001 <www.yourlibrary.ws/ya_webpage/ritba/ritba04/ritba04.htm> 6-12

SPONSOR: Rhode Island Education Media Association, Rhode Island Library Association

PURPOSE: To promote quality young adult literature and promote teen participation in highlighting award-winning books.

NAME ORIGIN: The name was chosen to be descriptive of the teens who read and vote for the award.

SELECTION CRITERIA: The books are nominated based on their literary quality and their appeal to teens by the Rhode Island Teen Book Award Committee. Approximately 20 titles are on the list.

VOTING: Teens must read three of the nominated titles to be eligible to vote.

2001	6-12	*Give a Boy a Gun* by Todd Strasser
2002	6-12	*The Sisterhood of the Traveling Pants* by Ann Brashares
2003	6-12	No Award Given

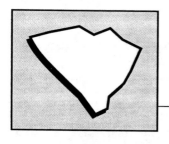

SOUTH CAROLINA

South Carolina Association of School Librarians' Book Award

1976   <www.scasl.net/BookAward/bkawrd.htm>   3-6 (Children's Book),
6-9 (Junior Book), 9-12 (Young Adult Book)

SPONSOR: South Carolina Association of School Librarians

PURPOSE: To encourage South Carolina students to read good quality contemporary literature and to honor the authors of the books annually chosen as the favorites by student vote.

SELECTION CRITERIA: Titles to be considered are nominated by members of the book award committees, with nominations sought and encouraged from students, teachers, librarians, and parents. Books may be fiction or nonfiction; should have good literary qualities (plot, characterization, narration, style); should reflect a balance of genre. Books included on each list should have appropriate content and interest levels for the specified grade levels. Award winners will not be considered. Books under consideration must have a copyright date of the present year or the preceding three years and be listed in the most current *Books in Print* or *Paperback Books in Print*. Each title must have at least one positive review from recognized reviewing sources by the organizational meeting and two reviews by the first voting meeting. Only one title by an author will be included on the final list, and there will be a three-year wait for an author to appear after that author has won any two South Carolina Book Awards. Every book need not be judged appropriate for each grade level, but books will be included for grades 3-6 (Children's), 6-9 (Junior), and 9-12 (Young Adult) with consideration of books with a reading level one grade below and one grade above the grades specified for the book award.

VOTING: Students are eligible to vote if they have read or heard three of the books from the list.

1976	3-6	*How to Eat Fried Worms* by Thomas Rockwell
1977	3-6	*Tales of a Fourth Grade Nothing* by Judy Blume
1978	3-6	*Otherwise Known as Sheila the Great* by Judy Blume

1979	3-6	*The Great Christmas Kidnaping Caper* by Jean Van Leeuwen
1980	3-6	*Shoeshine Girl* by Clyde Robert Bulla
	9-12	*The Amityville Horror* by Jay Anson
1981	3-6	*Bunnicula: A Rabbit Tale of Mystery* by James Howe
	9-12	*A Shining Season* by William J. Buchanan
1982	3-6	*The Ghost of Tillie Jean Cassaway* by Ellen Harvey Showell
	9-12	*The Boy Who Drank Too Much* by Shep Greene
1983	3-6	*Prisoners at the Kitchen Table* by Barbara Holland
	9-12	*About David* by Susan Beth Pfeffer
1984	3-6	*Jelly Belly* by Robert Kimmel Smith
	9-12	*Stranger With My Face* by Lois Duncan
1985	3-6	*The Monster's Ring* by Bruce Coville
	9-12	*The Divorce Express* by Paula Danziger
1986	3-6	*The War With Grandpa* by Robert Kimmel Smith
	9-12	*A String of Chances* by Phyllis Reynolds Naylor
1987	3-6	*Cracker Jackson* by Betsy Byars
	9-12	*If This Is Love, I'll Take Spaghetti* by Ellen Conford
1988	3-6	*Baby-sitting Is a Dangerous Job* by Willo Davis Roberts
	9-12	*Locked in Time* by Lois Duncan
1989	3-6	*Ferret in the Bedroom, Lizards in the Fridge* by Bill Wallace
	9-12	*Face at the Edge of the World* by Eve Bunting
1990	3-6	*Class Clown* by Johanna Hurwitz
	9-12	*The Year Without Michael* by Susan Beth Pfeffer
1991	3-6	*Is Anybody There?* by Eve Bunting
	9-12	*Fallen Angels* by Walter Dean Myers
1992	3-6	*Snot Stew* by Bill Wallace
	9-12	*On the Devil's Court* by Carl Deuker
1993	3-6	*Muggie Maggie* by Beverly Cleary
	6-9	*The Dead Man in Indian Creek* by Mary Downing Hahn
	9-12	*The Silver Kiss* by Annette Curtis Klause
1994	3-6	*Fourth Grade Rats* by Jerry Spinelli
	6-9	*Stepping on the Cracks* by Mary Downing Hahn
	9-12	*Jurassic Park* by Michael Crichton
1995	3-6	*Sukey and the Mermaid* by Robert D. San Souci
	6-9	*A Ghost in the House* by Betty Ren Wright
	9-12	*What You Don't Know Can Kill You* by Fran Arrick
1996	3-6	*Stellaluna* by Janell Cannon
	6-9	*Baby* by Patricia MacLachlan
	9-12	*Detour for Emmy* by Marilyn Reynolds
1997	3-6	*The Best School Year Ever* by Barbara Robinson
	6-9	*Phoenix Rising* by Karen Hesse
	9-12	*Harris and Me: A Summer Remembered* by Gary Paulsen

1998	3-6	*The Story of Ruby Bridges* by Robert Coles
	6-9	*Mick Harte Was Here* by Barbara Park
	9-12	*A Time for Dancing* by Davida Wills Hurwin
1999	3-6	*Tornado* by Betsy Byars
	6-9	*Crash* by Jerry Spinelli
	9-12	*Slam!* by Walter Dean Myers
2000	3-6	*Rumpelstiltskin's Daughter* by Diane Stanley
	6-9	*Tangerine* by Edward Bloor
	9-12	*Blood and Chocolate* by Annette Curtis Klause
2001	3-6	*Thank You, Mr. Falker* by Patricia Polacco
	6-9	*Harry Potter and the Sorcerer's Stone* by J. K. Rowling
	9-12	*Someone Like You* by Sarah Dessen
2002	3-6	*Hooway for Wodney Wat!* by Helen Lester
	6-9	*Dork in Disguise* by Carol Gorman
	9-12	*Speak* by Laurie Halse Anderson
2003	3-6	*Because of Winn-Dixie* by Kate DiCamillo
	6-9	*Jade Green: A Ghost Story* by Joan Lowery Nixon
	9-12	*The Body of Christopher Creed* by Carol Plum-Ucci

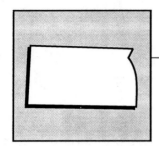

SOUTH DAKOTA

Prairie Bud Award
1998   <www.sdstatelibrary.com/forkids/prairie/index.htm>   K-3

SPONSOR: Public Library and Trustee Section and School Library and Media Section of the South Dakota Library Association, South Dakota Reading Council, South Dakota State Library, South Dakota Elementary School Principals

PURPOSE: To encourage children to become enthusiastic, discriminating readers.

NAME ORIGIN: Named after the early stage of the state flower, the Pasque flower, thus the name Prairie Bud.

SELECTION CRITERIA: Books must meet these requirements: book titles, not authors are selected; be fiction and nonfiction titles; be published two to three years prior to the voting year; be in print; be written by living American authors; and reflect children's reading choices. TV or movie tie-ins are not allowed. Books must meet regular library selection standards; must be chosen because of suitability and overall interest to children; and illustrations must be artistic and suitable. Teachers and librarians may recommend books appropriate for children in kindergarten through third grade.

VOTING: Any South Dakota student in kindergarten through grade three may participate. To vote, a child must read or hear at least five of the nominated books. Students may only vote for a book that they have read or heard.

1998	K-3	*The Toll-Bridge Troll* by Patricia Rae Wolff. Kimberly Bulcken Root, ill.
1999	K-3	*My Little Sister Ate One Hare* by Bill Grossman. Kevin Hawkes, ill.
2000	K-3	*Rotten Teeth* by Laura Simms. David Catrow, ill.
2001	K-3	*Look-Alikes* by Joan Steiner. Thomas Lindley, ill.
2002	K-3	No Award Given
2003	K-3	*Baby Beebee Bird* by Diane Redfield Massie. Steven Kellogg, ill.

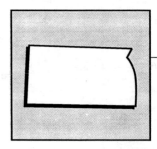

SOUTH DAKOTA

Prairie Pasque Award

1987   <www.sdstatelibrary.com/forkids/prairie/index.htm>   4-6

SPONSOR: Public Library and Trustee Section and School Library and Media Section of the South Dakota Library Association, South Dakota Reading Council, South Dakota State Library, South Dakota Elementary School Principals

PURPOSE: To encourage children to become enthusiastic, discriminating readers.

NAME ORIGIN: Named after the state flower—Pasque flower.

SELECTION CRITERIA: Books must meet these requirements: book titles, not authors are selected; be fiction and nonfiction titles; be published two to three years prior to the voting year; be in print; be written by living American authors; and reflect children's reading choices. TV or movie tie-ins are not allowed. Books must meet regular library selection standards; must be chosen because of suitability and overall interest to children; and illustrations must be artistic and suitable. Teachers and librarians may recommend books appropriate for children in grades four through six.

VOTING: Fourth, fifth, and sixth grade students who read or hear at least five books from the list are eligible to vote. A student can only vote for a book that they have read or heard.

1987	4-6	*Night of the Twisters* by Ivy Ruckman
1988	4-6	*Switcharound* by Lois Lowry
1989	4-6	*A Royal Pain* by Ellen Conford
1990	4-6	*This Island Isn't Big Enough for the Four of Us* by Gery Greer and Bob Ruddick
1991	4-6	*All About Sam* by Lois Lowry
1992	4-6	*The Doll in the Garden: A Ghost Story* by Mary Downing Hahn
1993	4-6	*Hugh Glass, Mountain Man* by Robert M. McClung
1994	4-6	*Shiloh* by Phyllis Reynolds Naylor
1995	4-6	*Devil's Bridge* by Cynthia DeFelice
1996	4-6	*Someone Was Watching* by David Patneaude
1997	4-6	*The Best School Year Ever* by Barbara Robinson
1998	4-6	*Titanic Crossing* by Barbara Williams

1999	4-6	*Frindle* by Andrew Clements
2000	4-6	*The Adventures of Captain Underpants: An Epic Novel* by Dav Pilkey
2001	4-6	*Holes* by Louis Sachar
2002	4-6	*Bud, Not Buddy* by Christopher Paul Curtis
2003	4-6	*Because of Winn-Dixie* by Kate DiCamillo

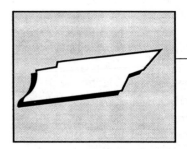

TENNESSEE

Volunteer State Book Award
1979 <www.mtsu.edu/~kpatten/vsba.
html> PreK-3, 4-6, 7-12

SPONSOR: Tennessee Library Association, Tennessee Association of School Librarians

PURPOSE: To promote awareness, interest, and enjoyment of good new children's and young adult literature. The award also hopes to promote literacy and lifelong reading habits by encouraging students to read quality contemporary literature, which broadens understanding of the human experience and provides accurate, factual information. This award will honor outstanding books chosen annually by Tennessee students.

NAME ORIGIN: Named after the state nickname—Volunteer State.

SELECTION CRITERIA: Professional librarians and educators who work continuously with students in kindergarten through twelfth grades select books appealing to students in each of three grade categories. The committees welcome nominations from participating schools. Books may be fiction or nonfiction and be published in the five years before the year of voting; textbooks, anthologies, translations, and books from foreign publishers are not eligible. Only one title of any one author will be included on the current list and only books by authors residing in the United States are eligible. All books on the final lists are read by a minimum of two members of the committee.

VOTING: Students who have read or heard a minimum of three of the nominated books in one age group are allowed to vote.

1979	*How to Eat Fried Worms* by Thomas Rockwell
1980	*Ramona and Her Father* by Beverly Cleary
1981	*Shadows* by Lynn Hall
1982	*Superfudge* by Judy Blume
1983	*The Cybil War* by Betsy Byars
1984	*Return to Howliday Inn* by James Howe
1985	*When the Boys Ran the House* by Joan Carris
1986	*Operation Dump the Chump* by Barbara Park
1987	*Skinnybones* by Barbara Park
1988	*The War With Grandpa* by Robert Kimmel Smith

1989	K-3	*In a Dark, Dark Room: and Other Scary Stories* by Alvin Schwartz. Dirk Zimmer, ill.
	4-6	*Wait Till Helen Comes* by Mary Downing Hahn
	7-9	*Dogsong: A Novel* by Gary Paulsen
	10-12	*Izzy, Willy-Nilly* by Cynthia Voigt
1990	K-3	*Abiyoyo* by Pete Seeger. Michael Hayes, ill.
	4-6	*Christina's Ghost* by Betty Ren Wright
	7-9	*Putting on an Act* by Christi Killien
	10-12	*Locked in Time* by Lois Duncan
1991	K-3	*The Magic School Bus at the Waterworks* by Joanna Cole. Bruce Degan, ill.
	4-6	*Beetles, Lightly Toasted* by Phyllis Reynolds Naylor
	7-9	*The Shadow Club* by Neal Shusterman
	10-12	*Say Goodnight, Gracie* by Julie Reece Deaver
1992	K-3	*No Jumping on the Bed!* by Tedd Arnold
	4-6	*There's a Boy in the Girls' Bathroom* by Louis Sachar
	7-9	*A Sudden Silence* by Eve Bunting
	10-12	*Don't Look Behind You* by Lois Duncan
1993	K-3	*Very Quiet Cricket* by Eric Carle
	4-6	*Wayside School Is Falling Down* by Louis Sachar
	7-9	*A Killing Freeze* by Lynn Hall
1994	K-3	*Tailypo!* by Jan Wahl. Wil Clay, ill.
	4-6	*Our Sixth-Grade Sugar Babies* by Eve Bunting
	7-12	*Don't Look Behind You* by Lois Duncan
1995	K-3	*Land of the Gray Wolf* by Thomas Locker
	4-6	*Fudge-A-Mania* by Judy Blume
	7-12	*The Face on the Milk Carton* by Caroline Cooney
1996	K-3	*The Three Little Wolves and the Big Bad Pig* by Eugene Trivizas. Helen Oxenbury, ill.
	4-6	*The Ghosts of Mercy Manor* by Betty Ren Wright
	7-12	*Heart of a Champion* by Carl Deuker
1997	K-3	*Dogzilla: Starring Flash, Rabies, Dwayne, and Introducing Leia as the Monster* by Dav Pilkey
	4-6	*The Best School Year Ever* by Barbara Robinson
	7-12	*Deadly Deception* by Betsy Haynes
1998	K-3	*Hallowiener* by Dav Pilkey
	4-6	*Help! I'm Trapped in My Teacher's Body* by Todd Strasser
	7-12	*Driver's Ed* by Caroline Cooney
1999	K-3	*Martha Calling* by Susan Meddaugh
	4-6	*Shiloh Season* by Phyllis Reynolds Naylor
	7-12	*Tears of a Tiger* by Sharon Draper
2000	K-3	*Parts* by Tedd Arnold

	4-6	*The Million Dollar Shot* by Dan Gutman
	7-12	*Brian's Winter* by Gary Paulsen
2001	K-3	*Pickin' Peas* by Margaret Read MacDonald. Pat Cummings, ill.
	4-6	*Holes* by Louis Sachar
	7-12	*Gallows Hill* by Lois Duncan
2002	K-3	*Hooway for Wodney Wat!* by Helen Lester. Lynn Munsinger, ill.
	4-6	*Bud, Not Buddy* by Christopher Paul Curtis
	7-12	*Smart Dog* by Vivian Vande Velde
	7-12	*Speak* by Laurie Halse Anderson
2003	K-3	*Cosmo Zooms* by Arthur Howard
	4-6	*Because of Winn-Dixie* by Kate DiCamillo
	7-12	*The Princess Diaries* by Meg Cabot

TEXAS

Texas Bluebonnet Award
1981   <www.txla.org/groups/tba/index.html>   3-6

SPONSOR: Texas Library Association Children's Round Table, Texas Association of School Librarians

PURPOSE: To encourage Texas children to read more books, explore a variety of current books, develop powers of discrimination, and identify their favorite books.

NAME ORIGIN: Named after the state flower—Bluebonnet.

SELECTION CRITERIA: The Texas Bluebonnet Award committee is responsible for selection of the books on each year's list with suggestions solicited from librarians, teachers, parents, students, and other interested persons. In selecting titles, the committee considers student interests, appropriate content, reputable reviews, literary quality, and reading level. Both fiction and nonfiction books are represented; authors must be a living U.S. citizen or one who resides and publishes in the United States. Books considered for the list must have been published in the United States within three years of the list release date. Textbooks, new editions, and abridgements are not eligible. The list contains 20 titles.

VOTING: Students must read or hear at least five of the current list titles to be eligible to vote.

1981	3-6	*Ramona and Her Father* by Beverly Cleary
1982	3-6	*Superfudge* by Judy Blume
1983	3-6	*A Dog Called Kitty* by Bill Wallace
1984	3-6	*Nothing's Fair in Fifth Grade* by Barthe DeClements
1985	3-6	*Skinnybones* by Barbara Park
1986	3-6	*The Dollhouse Murders* by Betty Ren Wright
1987	3-6	*Hot and Cold Summer* by Johanna Hurwitz
1988	3-6	*Christina's Ghost* by Betty Ren Wright
1989	3-6	*Wait Till Helen Comes* by Mary Downing Hahn
1990	3-6	*There's a Boy in the Girls' Bathroom* by Louis Sachar
1991	3-6	*Aliens for Breakfast* by Jonathan Etra and Stephanie Spinner
1992	3-6	*Snot Stew* by Bill Wallace

1993	3-6	*The Houdini Box* by Brian Selznick
1994	3-6	*Shiloh* by Phyllis Reynolds Naylor
1995	3-6	*The Stinky Cheese Man and Other Fairly Stupid Tales* by Jon Scieszka
1996	3-6	*Time for Andrew: A Ghost Story* by Mary Downing Hahn
1997	3-6	*Math Curse* by Jon Scieszka
1998	3-6	*Tornado* by Betsy Byars
1999	3-6	*Verdi* by Janell Cannon
2000	3-6	*The Ghost of Fossil Glen* by Cynthia DeFelice
2001	3-6	*Cook-a-Doodle-Doo!* by Janet Stevens and Susan Stevens Crummel
2002	3-6	*Because of Winn-Dixie* by Kate DiCamillo
2003	3-6	*The Golden Mare, the Firebird, and the Magic Ring: A Folktale With a Twist* by Ruth Sanderson
2003	3-6	*Shoeless Joe and Black Betsy* by Phil Bildner

UTAH

Beehive Awards
1980 <www.clau.org/> K-3 (Picture Book),
3-6 (Children's Fiction), 3-6 N (Informational),
P (K-6 Poetry), 7-12 (Young Adult)

SPONSOR: Children's Literature Association of Utah

PURPOSE: To motivate reading.

NAME ORIGIN: Named after the state nickname—Beehive State.

SELECTION CRITERIA: The lists have five to 15 titles which must be appropriate for the intended grade level; be in print; be published within five years (three years for informational books) prior to being on the list; have favorable reviews in professional review journals. Books are evaluated in regard to originality, artistic worth, content, appeal, literary quality, and imagination. The list strives for a balance of reading levels, genres, subject areas, interest, and appeal. Award winners are not eligible, and only one title per author is allowed. After appearing on the final list, the books are excluded from appearing again.

VOTING: No set number of titles is required for voting, but children are encouraged to read as many titles as possible.

1980	3-6	*Ramona and Her Father* by Beverly Cleary
1981	3-6	*The Letter, the Witch, and the Ring* by John Bellairs
	3-6	*Eddie's Menagerie* by Carolyn Haywood
1982	3-6	*Superfudge* by Judy Blume
1983	3-6	*The Chocolate Touch* by Patrick Catling
1984	3-6	*Lost in the Devil's Desert* by Gloria Skurzynski
1985	3-6	*Stone Fox* by John Gardiner
1986	3-6	*Me and the Weirdos* by Jane Sutton
	3-6 N	*Great Painters* by Piero Ventura
1987	3-6	*Skinnybones* by Barbara Park
	3-6 N	No Award Given
1988	3-6	*Wait Till Helen Comes* by Mary Downing Hahn
	3-6 N	*How Much Is a Million?* by David Schwartz
1989	3-6	*Trapped in Death Cave* by Bill Wallace
	3-6 N	*Your Amazing Senses: 36 Games, Puzzles and Tricks That Show How Your Senses Work* by Ron Van Der Meer

1990	3-6	*This Island Isn't Big Enough for the Four of Us* by Gery Greer and Bob Ruddick
	3-6 N	*How to Make Pop-Ups* by Joan Irvine
1991	3-6	*Matilda* by Roald Dahl
	3-6 N	*Bill Peet: An Autobiography* by Bill Peet
1992	3-6	*There's a Boy in the Girls' Bathroom* by Louis Sachar
	3-6 N	*An Ant Colony* by Heiderose Fischer-Nagel
	7-12	*Don't Look Behind You* by Lois Duncan
1993	3-6	*The Dead Man in Indian Creek* by Mary Downing Hahn
	3-6 N	*Dolphin Adventure: A True Story* by Wayne Grover
	7-12	*Sniper* by Theodore Taylor
1994	3-6	*Jeremy Thatcher, Dragon Hatcher* by Bruce Coville
	3-6 N	*Stephen Biesty's Incredible Cross-Sections* by Richard Platt
	7-12	*The True Confessions of Charlotte Doyle* by Avi
1995	3-6	*The Ghosts of Mercy Manor* by Betty Ren Wright
	3-6 N	*Sadako* by Eleanor Coerr
	7-12	*Amazing Gracie* by A. E. Cannon
1996	K-3	*Two of Everything: A Chinese Folktale* by Lily Toy Hong
	3-6	*Time for Andrew: A Ghost Story* by Mary Downing Hahn
	3-6 N	*Mummies and Their Mysteries* by Charlotte Wilcox
	7-12	*Nothing to Fear* by Jackie French Koller
1997	K-*3*	*A Job for Wittilda* by Caralyn Buehner. Mark Buehner, ill.
	3-6	*Watchdog and the Coyotes* by Bill Wallace
	3-6 N	*Never Take a Pig to Lunch: Poems About the Fun of Eating* by Nadine Bernard Westcott
	7-12	*In My Father's House* by Ann Rinaldi
1998	K-3	*Anansi and the Talking Melon* by Eric Kimmel. Janet Stevens, ill.
	3-6	*Someone Was Watching* by David Patneaude
	3-6 N	*It's a Spoon, Not a Shovel* by Caralyn Buehner
	7-12	*The Merlin Effect* by T. A. Barron
1999	K-3	*Watch Out! Big Bro's Coming!* by Jez Alborough
	3-6	*Earthquake Terror* by Peg Kehret
	3-6 N	*Passage to Freedom: The Sugihara Story* by Ken Mochizuki
	7-12	*SOS Titanic* by Eve Bunting
2000	K-3	*A Bad Case of Stripes* by David Shannon
	3-6	*Frindle* by Andrew Clements
	3-6 N	*A Drop of Water: A Book of Science and Wonder* by Walter Wick
	7-12	*Little Sister* by Kara Dalkey
2001	K-3	*Hooway for Wodney Wat!* by Helen Lester. Lynn Munsinger, ill.
	3-6	*The Secret of Platform 13* by Eva Ibbotson
	3-6 N	*If You Hopped Like a Frog* by David Schwartz

	7-12	*A Long Way From Chicago: A Novel in Stories* by Richard Peck
2002	K-3	*Sitting Ducks* by Michael Bedard
	3-6	*Midnight Magic* by Avi
	3-6 N	*The Snake Scientist* by Sy Montgomery
	7-12	*Downsiders* by Neal Shusterman
	P	*Insectlopedia: Poems and Paintings* by Douglas Florian
2003	K-3	*Stand Tall, Molly Lou Melon* by Patty Lovell. David Catrow, ill.
	3-6	*The Two Princesses of Bamarre* by Gail Carson Levine
	3-6 N	*Tiger Math: Learning to Graph from a Baby Tiger* by Ann Whitehead Nagda and Cindy Bickel
	7-12	*Touching Spirit Bear* by Ben Mikaelsen
	P	*Take Me Out of the Bathtub and Other Silly Dilly Songs* by Alan Katz. David Catrow, ill.

VERMONT

Dorothy Canfield Fisher Children's Book Award
1957   <www.dcfaward.org/>   4-8

SPONSOR: Vermont Department of Libraries, Vermont Parent Teachers Association

PURPOSE: To encourage Vermont school children to become enthusiastic and discriminating readers.

NAME ORIGIN: Vermont author, Dorothy Canfield Fisher, felt that reading from the earliest years was one of the greatest influences on character development. To honor her understanding of the human spirit and her many years promoting the tradition of individual freedom, the award was named for her.

SELECTION CRITERIA: The committee considers books of fiction, information, and poetry that are of commendable quality, exhibit creativity, reflect students' interests, and will increase their enjoyment of reading. To be eligible for the list books should be published in the preceding calendar year. Reprints and compilations previously copyrighted are not eligible. Books must be written by a living author who is a citizen or resident of the United States; co-authors may be included. Books must be original or, if traditional in origin, the result of individual research. Any retelling and reinterpretation must be the writer's own. Poetry, anthologies, and short stories must be by a single author and not previously copyrighted. Books written by a previous recipient of the *Dorothy Canfield Fisher Award* may be considered at the discretion of the committee. Books should have children as their intended audience, display respect for children's understanding, ability and appreciation, and be appropriate for students in grades four through eight. The list consists of 30 books.

VOTING: Children in grades four through eight should vote for their favorite book and may vote for only one book. It is not necessary to have read all the books in order to vote, but the committee recommends that children read at least five so that they are able to select a true "favorite" from the list.

1957	4-8	*Old Bones, the Wonder Horse* by Mildred Pace
1958	4-8	*Fifteen* by Beverly Cleary
1959	4-8	*Comanche of the Seventh* by Margaret Leighton
1960	4-8	*Double or Nothing* by Phoebe Erickson
1961	4-8	*Captain Ghost* by Thelma Harrington Bell
1962	4-8	*City Under the Back Steps* by Evelyn Sibley Lampman
1963	4-8	*The Incredible Journey* by Sheila Burnford
1964	4-8	*Bristle Face* by Zachary Ball
1965	4-8	*Rascal* by Sterling North
1966	4-8	*Ribsy* by Beverly Cleary
1967	4-8	*The Summer I Was Lost* by Phillip Viereck
1968	4-8	*The Taste of Spruce Gum* by Jacqueline Jackson
1969	4-8	*Two in the Wilderness* by Mary Wolfe Thompson
1970	4-8	*Kavik, the Wolf Dog* by Walt Morey
1971	4-8	*Go to the Room of the Eyes* by Betty K. Erwin
1972	4-8	*Flight of the White Wolf* by Mel Ellis
1973	4-8	*Never Steal a Magic Cat* by Don and Joan Caufield
1974	4-8	*Catch a Killer* by George A. Woods
1975	4-8	*The 18th Emergency* by Betsy Byars
1976	4-8	*The Toothpaste Millionaire* by Jean Merrill
1977	4-8	*A Smart Kid Like You* by Stella Pevsner
1978	4-8	*Summer of Fear* by Lois Duncan
1979	4-8	*Kid Power* by Susan Beth Pfeffer
1980	4-8	*Bones on Black Spruce Mountain* by David Budbill
1981	4-8	*Bunnicula: A Rabbit Tale of Mystery* by James Howe
1982	4-8	*The Hand-Me-Down Kid* by Francine Pascal
1983	4-8	*Tiger Eyes* by Judy Blume
1984	4-8	*A Bundle of Sticks* by Pat Rhoads Mauser
1985	4-8	*Dear Mr. Henshaw* by Beverly Cleary
1986	4-8	*The War With Grandpa* by Robert Kimmel Smith
1987	4-8	*The Castle in the Attic* by Elizabeth Winthrop
1988	4-8	*Wait Till Helen Comes* by Mary Downing Hahn
1989	4-8	*Hatchet* by Gary Paulsen
1990	4-8	*Where It Stops, Nobody Knows* by Amy Ehrlich
1991	4-8	*Number the Stars* by Lois Lowry
1992	4-8	*Maniac Magee* by Jerry Spinelli
1993	4-8	*Shiloh* by Phyllis Reynolds Naylor
1994	4-8	*Jennifer Murdley's Toad: A Magic Shop Book* by Bruce Coville
1995	4-8	*The Boggart* by Susan Cooper
1996	4-8	*Time for Andrew: A Ghost Story* by Mary Downing Hahn
1997	4-8	*Mick Harte Was Here* by Barbara Park
1998	4-8	*Small Steps: The Year I Got Polio* by Peg Kehret

1999	4-8	*Ella Enchanted* by Gail Carson Levine
2000	4-8	*Holes* by Louis Sachar
2001	4-8	*Bud, Not Buddy* by Christopher Paul Curtis
2002	4-8	*Because of Winn-Dixie* by Kate DiCamillo
2003	4-8	*Love That Dog* by Sharon Creech

VERMONT

Red Clover Award, Vermont's Children's Choice Picture Book Award
1997   <www.vermontbook.org/Red-Clover.html>
K-4

SPONSOR: Mother Goose Programs, Windham County Reads, Vermont Department of Education, Vermont Department of Libraries

PURPOSE: To promote the reading and discussion of the best of contemporary picture books.

NAME ORIGIN: Named after the state flower—Red Clover.

SELECTION CRITERIA: Titles must have an American author and illustrator (or the same person)—alive and living in the United States, and be published during the year of consideration for next year's list. Only one title by the same combination of author and illustrator during a given year is considered. Books appropriate for the age group (kindergarten through grade four) in both fiction and nonfiction are considered.

VOTING: Students must read or hear at least five titles to be eligible to vote.

1997	K-4	*Piggie Pie* by Margie Palatini. Howard Fine, ill.
1998	K-4	*Art Dog* by Thacher Hurd
1999	K-4	*Akiak: A Tale from the Iditarod* by Robert J. Blake
2000	K-4	*Ten Minutes Till Bedtime* by Peggy Rathman
2001	K-4	*Bark, George* by Jules Feiffer
2002	K-4	*Click, Clack, Moo: Cows That Type* by Doreen Cronin. Betsy Lewin, ill.
2003	K-4	*Baloney, Henry P.* by Jon Scieszka. Lane Smith, ill.

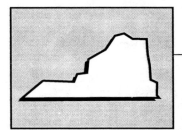

VIRGINIA

Virginia Young Readers Award
1982 <www.vsra.org/Vyrpindex.html>
or <www.vsra.org/Virginia_Young_Readers.
html> K-3 (Primary), 3-6 (Elementary), 6-8 (Middle), 9-12 (High)

SPONSOR: Virginia State Reading Association, Virginia Educational
Media Association, Virginia Library Association, Library of Virginia
Youth Services

PURPOSE: To encourage young readers to become better acquainted with
contemporary books with outstanding literary appeal; to broaden students'
awareness of literature as a lifelong pleasure; to encourage reading aloud in
classrooms as a means of introducing reading for pleasure; and to honor
favorite books and their authors.

SELECTION CRITERIA: The book must be published within five years
before the ballot on which it appears. Additionally, books must be age
appropriate for the list on which they appear.

VOTING: To become a qualified voter, a participant must read or hear at
least four of the nominated books at each level in their entirety. Students
may vote in more than one level as long as they have met the requirement
for each level.

1982	3-6	*Island of the Blue Dolphins* by Scott O'Dell
1983	3-6	*Bridge to Terabithia* by Katherine Paterson
1984	3-6	No Award Given
	6-8	*The Westing Game* by Ellen Raskin
1985	3-6	No Award Given
	6-8	No Award Given
	9-12	*The Outsiders* by S. E. Hinton
1986	3-6	*Superfudge* by Judy Blume
	6-8	*The Cat Ate My Gymsuit* by Paula Danziger
	9-12	*The Third Eye* by Mollie Hunter
1987	3-6	*My Friend, the Vampire* by Angela Sommer-Bodenburg
	6-8	*The Curse of the Blue Figurine* by John Bellairs
	9-12	*The Man in the Woods* by Rosemary Wells
1988	K-3	*In a Dark, Dark Room: and Other Scary Stories* by Alvin Schwartz. Dirk Zimmer, ill.

	3-6	*The Indian in the Cupboard* by Lynne Reid Banks
	6-8	*Ghost in My Soup* by Judi Miller
	9-12	*Izzy, Willy-Nilly* by Cynthia Voigt
1989	K-3	*Heckedy Peg* by Audrey Wood. Don Wood, ill.
	3-6	*Wait Till Helen Comes* by Mary Downing Hahn
	6-8	*The Other Side of Dark* by Joan Lowery Nixon
	9-12	*Face at the Edge of the World* by Eve Bunting
1990	K-3	*The Magic School Bus Inside the Earth* by Joanna Cole
	3-6	*Christina's Ghost* by Betty Ren Wright
	6-8	*Hatchet* by Gary Paulsen
	9-12	*Wolf Rider: A Tale of Terror* by Avi
1991	K-3	*Two Bad Ants* by Chris Van Allsburg
	3-6	*Matilda* by Roald Dahl
	6-8	*Good Night, Mr. Tom* by Michelle Magorian
	9-12	*Say Goodnight, Gracie* by Julie Reece Deaver
1992	K-3	*The Great White Man-Eating Shark: A Cautionary Tale* by Margaret Mahy. Jonathan Allen, ill.
	3-6	*The Doll in the Garden: A Ghost Story* by Mary Downing Hahn
	6-8	*A Family Apart* by Joan Lowery Nixon
	9-12	*Don't Look Behind You* by Lois Duncan
1993	K-3	*The Talking Eggs: A Folktale from the American South* by Robert D. San Souci. Jerry Pinkney, ill.
	3-6	*Exploring the Titanic* by Robert Ballard
	6-8	*Maniac Magee* by Jerry Spinelli
	9-12	*Plague Year* by Stephanie Tolan
1994	K-3	*Beware of Boys* by Tony Blundell
	3-6	*Ten Kids, No Pets* by Ann M. Martin
	6-8	*The Dead Man in Indian Creek* by Mary Downing Hahn
	9-12	*How Could You Do It, Diane?* by Stella Pevsner
1995	K-3	*The Rough-Face Girl* by Rafe Martin. David Shannon, ill.
	3-6	*The Ghost Cadet* by Elaine Alphin
	6-8	*Flight #116 Is Down* by Caroline Cooney
	9-12	*Jumping the Nail* by Eve Bunting
1996	K-3	*Dogzilla: Starring Flash, Rabies, Dwayne, and Introducing Leia as the Monster* by Dav Pilkey
	3-6	*A Haunting in Williamsburg* by Lou Kassem
	6-8	*The Giver* by Lois Lowry
	9-12	*Just Like Martin* by Ossie Davis
1997	K-3	*Copycat* by Ruth Brown
	3-6	*Time for Andrew: A Ghost Story* by Mary Downing Hahn
	6-8	*Walk Two Moons* by Sharon Creech
	9-12	*Tears of a Tiger* by Sharon Draper

1998	K-3	*Suddenly!* by Colin McNaughton
	3-6	*Fig Pudding* by Ralph Fletcher
	6-8	*The Ear, the Eye, and the Arm* by Nancy Farmer
	9-12	*Daughter of the Stars* by Phyllis A. Whitney
1999	K-3	*My Little Sister Ate One Hare* by Bill Grossman. Kevin Hawkes, ill.
	3-6	*Earthquake Terror* by Peg Kehret
	6-8	*Crash* by Jerry Spinelli
	9-12	*The China Garden* by Liz Berry
2000		No Award Given
2001	K-3	*Akiak: A Tale from the Iditarod* by Robert J. Blake
	3-6	*The Ghost of Fossil Glen* by Cynthia DeFelice
	6-8	*Joey Pigza Swallowed the Key* by Jack Gantos
	9-12	*If You Come Softly* by Jacqueline Woodson
2002	K-3	*Hooway for Wodney Wat!* by Helen Lester. Lynn Munsinger, ill.
	3-6	*The Secret of Platform 13* by Eva Ibbotson
	6-8	*Blackwater* by Eve Bunting
	9-12	*A Door Near Here* by Heather Quarles
2003	K-3	*Soccer Mom From Outer Space* by Barney Saltzberg
	3-6	*Because of Winn-Dixie* by Kate DiCamillo
	6-8	*No More Dead Dogs* by Gordon Korman
	9-12	*Angus, Thongs and Full Frontal Snogging: Confessions of Georgia Nicolson* by Louise Rennison

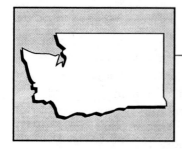

WASHINGTON

Evergreen Young Adult Book Award

1991   <www.kcls.org/evergreen/>   7-12

SPONSOR: Washington State Young Adult Review Group

PURPOSE: To encourage teenagers to read and discuss new fiction and nonfiction materials relevant to their lives.

NAME ORIGIN: Named after the state nickname—Evergreen State.

SELECTION CRITERIA: Exceptional titles published three years before the award date are suggested to the nominating committee. Teachers, students, parents, or librarians can make nominations.

VOTING: Students must be in grades seven through twelve and have read at least three of the nominees to be eligible to vote.

1991	7-12	*Seventh Son* by Orson Scott Card
1992	7-12	*Creature* by John Saul
1993	7-12	*The True Confessions of Charlotte Doyle* by Avi
1994	7-12	*Say Goodnight, Gracie* by Julie Reece Deaver
1995	7-12	*The Pelican Brief* by John Grisham
1995	7-12	*Flight #116 Is Down* by Caroline Cooney
1996	7-12	*The Client* by John Grisham
1997	7-12	*Driver's Ed* by Caroline Cooney
1998	7-12	*The Hot Zone* by Richard Preston
1999	7-12	*Nathan's Run* by John Gilstrap
2000	7-12	*Chicken Soup for the Teenage Soul: 101 Stories of Life, Love and Learning*
2001	7-12	*Holes* by Louis Sachar
2002	7-12	*Speak* by Laurie Halse Anderson
2003	7-12	*The Princess Diaries* by Meg Cabot

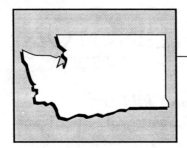

WASHINGTON

Sasquatch Reading Award
1998   <www.wlma.org/Association/
sasquatch. htm>   4-8

SPONSOR: Washington Library Media Association

PURPOSE: To encourage children, between emerging and intermediate reading levels, to read for pleasure. The award fills the gap not covered by the *Washington Children's Choice Picture Book Award*, and the *Young Reader's Choice Award*.

NAME ORIGIN: It was thought that the Sasquatch, a mythical creature that purportedly lives in the wilderness areas of Washington State, was a recognizable and whimsical icon.

SELECTION CRITERIA: Students, teachers, or librarians may make nominations. Books for the 2005 list had a 2001 through 2002 copyright.

VOTING: Children must read or hear at least two titles to be eligible to vote.

1998	4-8	*Mick Harte Was Here* by Barbara Park
1999	4-8	*Frindle* by Andrew Clements
2000	4-8	*Harry Potter and the Sorcerer's Stone* by J. K. Rowling
2001	4-8	*Joey Pigza Swallowed the Key* by Jack Gantos
2002	4-8	*Dork in Disguise* by Carol Gorman
2003	4-8	*Because of Winn-Dixie* by Kate DiCamillo

WASHINGTON

Washington Children's Choice Picture Book Award
1982   <www.wlma.org/Association/wccpba. htm>   K-3

SPONSOR: Washington Library Media Association

PURPOSE: To experience a wide variety of picture books.

SELECTION CRITERIA: Books selected must be from titles published one to two years before the award year; be in picture book format; be either nonfiction or fiction, and may include photography and wordless books. The current year's winning book is not eligible for nomination, but there is no restriction on re-nominating the non-winners. Books are to be in print, and distributed in the United States. The list will contain no more than 20 titles.

VOTING: Students listen to their school librarian or classroom teacher read all of the titles. Students then vote for only one favorite nominee.

1982	K-3	*Cross-Country Cat* by Mary Calhoun. Erick Ingraham, ill.
1983	K-3	*Space Case* by Edward Marshall. James Marshall, ill.
1984	K-3	*Jumanji* by Chris Van Allsburg
1985	K-3	*Nimby* by Jasper Tomkins
1986	K-3	*The Unicorn and the Lake* by Marianna Mayer. Michael Hague, ill.
1987	K-3	*In a Dark, Dark Room: and Other Scary Stories* by Alvin Schwartz. Dirk Zimmer, ill.
1988	K-3	*King Bidgood's in the Bathtub* by Audrey Wood. Don Wood, ill.
1989	K-3	*The Magic School Bus at the Waterworks* by Joanna Cole. Bruce Degan, ill.
1990	K-3	*Amos: The Story of an Old Dog and His Couch* by Susan Seligson and Howie Schneider
1991	K-3	*Two Bad Ants* by Chris Van Allsburg
1992	K-3	*Hershel and the Hanukkah Goblins* by Eric Kimmel. Trina Schart Hyman, ill.
1993	K-3	*The Great White Man-Eating Shark: A Cautionary Tale* by Margaret Mahy. Jonathan Allen, ill.

1994	K-3	*The Dog Who Had Kittens* by Polly M. Robertus. Janet Stevens, ill.
1995	K-3	*Tiger* by Judy Allen. Tudor Humphries, ill.
1996	K-3	*Soap! Soap! Don't Forget the Soap!* by Tom Birdseye. Andrew Glass, ill.
1997	K-3	*Harvey Potter's Balloon Farm* by Jerdine Nolen. Mark Buehner, ill.
1998	K-3	*Heart of a Tiger* by Marsha Diane Arnold. Jamichael Henterly, ill.
1999	K-3	*Secret Shortcut* by Mark Teague
2000	K-3	*Akiak: A Tale from the Iditarod* by Robert J. Blake
2001	K-3	*Hooway for Wodney Wat!* by Helen Lester. Lynn Munsinger, ill.
2002	K-3	*Cosmo Zooms* by Arthur Howard
2003	K-3	*Widget* by Lyn Rossiter McFarland. Jim McFarland, ill.

WASHINGTON

See Pacific Northwest

WEST VIRGINIA

West Virginia Children's Book Award
1985   <www.wvcba.org>   3-6

SPONSOR: The West Virginia Children's Book Award Committee is a non-profit group of teachers, library media specialists, parents and other educators, with support from organizations such as the West Virginia Department of Education, West Virginia University, the West Virginia Library Association and Library Commission, RESA VII, and West Virginia Public Television.

PURPOSE: To introduce students to books that add to children's knowledge and enrich their understanding of the world; to increase their awareness and appreciation of varied cultures and social patterns; and to experience adventures and activities that are not possible in their own lives.

SELECTION CRITERIA: Books must be fiction; published in the United States in the last three years and in print. Textbooks, new editions, reprints, adaptations and abridgements are not eligible. Books should contain literary excellence and appropriateness of content.

VOTING: Students may vote for their favorite book.

1985	3-6	*Jumanji* by Chris Van Allsburg
1986	3-6	*Mustard* by Charlotte Graeber
1987	3-6	*Ralph S. Mouse* by Beverly Cleary
1988	3-6	*Herbie Jones* by Suzy Kline
1989	3-6	*Class Clown* by Johanna Hurwitz
1990	3-6	*Fudge* by Charlotte Graeber
1991	3-6	*There's a Boy in the Girls' Bathroom* by Louis Sachar
1992	3-6	*Matilda* by Roald Dahl
1993	3-6	*Maniac Magee* by Jerry Spinelli
1994	3-6	*Shiloh* by Phyllis Reynolds Naylor
1995	3-6	*Taxi Cat and Huey* by Gen LeRoy
1996	3-6	*The Boys Start the War* by Phyllis Reynolds Naylor
1997	3-6	*Nasty, Stinky Sneakers* by Eve Bunting
1998	3-6	*Earthquake Terror* by Peg Kehret
1999	3-6	*On Board the Titanic* by Shelley Tanaka
2000	3-6	*The Adventures of Captain Underpants: An Epic Novel* by Dav Pilkey

2001	3-6	*Harry Potter and the Sorcerer's Stone* by J. K. Rowling
2002	3-6	*Dork in Disguise* by Carol Gorman
2003	3-6	*Because of Winn-Dixie* by Kate DiCamillo

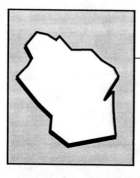

WISCONSIN

Golden Archer Award
1974 <www.wemaonline.org/cm.archer.cfm>
K-3 (Primary), 3-6 (Intermediate), 6-8
(Middle/Junior High)

SPONSOR: Wisconsin Educational Media Association

PURPOSE: To capture children's enthusiasm for reading, and to be used as a vehicle to introduce and encourage exposure to great literature.

NAME ORIGIN: The title of the award takes its inspiration from that bit of Longfellow verse: "I shot an arrow into the air; it fell to earth I know not where." The author, who captures the children's enthusiasm, is the "golden archer" deserving this award.

SELECTION CRITERIA: Books selected are recognized as noteworthy and of special interest to students; in print and readily available; published within the last five years; fiction or nonfiction; individual book titles, no series.

VOTING: There is no required number of books to read for voting eligibility.

1974-1992	K-3L	*Little Archer Award,* 4-8 *Original Golden Archer Award*
1974	4-8	*Are You There, God? It's Me, Margaret* by Judy Blume
1975	4-8	*How to Eat Fried Worms* by Thomas Rockwell
1976	K-3L	*The Funny Little Woman* by Arlene Mosel. Blair Lent, ill.
	4-8	*The Mystery of the Bewitched Bookmobile* by Florence Parry Heide
1977	K-3L	*Cyrus, the Unsinkable Sea Serpent* by Bill Peet
	4-8	*Ramona the Brave* by Beverly Cleary
1978	K-3L	*Oh, Were They Ever Happy!* by Peter Spier
	4-8	*The Home Run Trick* by Scott Corbett
1979	K-3L	*The Sweet Touch* by Lorna Balian
	4-8	*Summer of the Monkeys* by Wilson Rawls
1980	K-3L	*Cross-Country Cat* by Mary Calhoun. Erick Ingraham, ill.
	4-8	*This School Is Driving Me Crazy* by Nat Hentoff
1981	K-3L	*Pinkerton, Behave!* by Steven Kellogg
	4-8	*The Pinballs* by Betsy Byars
1982	K-3L	*Henry and the Red Stripes* by Eileen Christelow
	4-8	*My Sister's Keeper* by Beverly Butler

1983	K-3L	*Doctor DeSoto* by William Steig
	4-8	*Tex* by S. E. Hinton
1984	K-3L	*The Butter Battle Book* by Dr. Seuss
	4-8	*Nothing's Fair in Fifth Grade* by Barthe DeClements
1985	K-3L	*What's Under My Bed?* by James Stevenson
	4-8	*Tornado!* by Hilary Milton
1986	K-3L	*Polar Express* by Chris Van Allsburg
	4-8	*Whalesong* by Robert Siegel
1987	K-3L	*King Bidgood's in the Bathtub* by Audrey Wood. Don Wood, ill.
	4-8	*The Whipping Boy* by Sid Fleischman
1988	K-3L	*Hey, Al!* by Arthur Yorinks. Richard Egielski, ill.
	4-8	*On My Honor* by Marion Dane Bauer
1989	K-3L	*Underwear!* by Mary Monsell. Lynn Munsinger, ill.
	4-8	*Hatchet* by Gary Paulsen
1990	K-3L	*The Tub People* by Pam Conrad. Richard Egielski, ill.
	4-8	*Number the Stars* by Lois Lowry
1991	K-3L	*Borreguita and the Coyote: A Tale From Ayutla, Mexico* by Verna Aardema
	4-8	*Maniac Magee* by Jerry Spinelli
1992	K-3L	*Easter Egg Farm* by Mary Jane Auch
	4-8	*Shiloh* by Phyllis Reynolds Naylor
1993-1995		No Awards Given
1996	K-3	*Jumanji* by Chris Van Allsburg
	3-6	*Where the Sidewalk Ends* by Shel Silverstein
	6-8	*The Giver* by Lois Lowry
1997	K-3	*Officer Buckle and Gloria* by Peggy Rathman
	3-6	*The Stinky Cheese Man and Other Fairly Stupid Tales* by Jon Scieszka
	6-8	*Harris and Me: A Summer Remembered* by Gary Paulsen
1998	K-3	*Junie B. Jones and the Stupid, Smelly Bus* by Barbara Park
	3-6	*Falling Up* by Shel Silverstein
	6-8	*Number the Stars* by Lois Lowry
1999	K-3	*Hallowiener* by Dav Pilkey
	3-6	*Wayside School Gets a Little Stranger* by Louis Sachar
	6-8	*Brian's Winter* by Gary Paulsen
2000	K-3	*A Bad Case of Stripes* by David Shannon
	3-6	*Crash* by Jerry Spinelli
	6-8	*Harry Potter and the Sorcerer's Stone* by J. K. Rowling
2001	K-3	*Fishing for Methuselah* by Roger Roth
	3-6	*Harry Potter and the Prisoner of Azkaban* by J. K. Rowling
	6-8	*Holes* by Louis Sachar

2002	K-3	*Shake Dem Halloween Bones* by W. Nikola-Lisa. Mike Reed, ill.
	3-6	*Chicken Soup for the Kids' Soul: 101 Stories of Courage, Hope and Laughter*
	6-8	*Harry Potter and the Goblet of Fire* by J. K. Rowling
2003	K-3	*The Shark God* by Rafe Martin. David Shannon, ill.
	3-6	*Because of Winn-Dixie* by Kate DiCamillo
	6-8	*Stormbreaker* by Anthony Horowitz

WYOMING

Buckaroo Book Award
1999 <www.wyla.org/buckaroo/index.shtml> K-3

SPONSOR: Wyoming State Reading Council, Wyoming Library Association

PURPOSE: To help children become acquainted with the best contemporary authors; to help children become aware of the qualities of good books; to accustom younger children to concepts of choice, critical reading, and voting procedures which will help them participate in choosing other book awards; to honor an author whose book has been enjoyed by Wyoming children.

SELECTION CRITERIA: The books may be fiction or nonfiction; must be in print and have a copyright date within the last five years; may be a picture book, easy to read book, a high interest-low vocabulary book, or an appropriate grade level chapter book. The book must not first have appeared as a movie or TV show. Books cannot be on the list two consecutive years and only one title per author will be included on each year's list.

VOTING: Students must read or hear a minimum of three books to be eligible to vote. Students vote for only one book.

1999	K-3	*Stellaluna* by Janell Cannon
2000	K-3	No Award Given
2001	K-3	*Hooway for Wodney Wat!* by Helen Lester. Lynn Munsinger, ill.
2002	K-3	*No, David!* by David Shannon
2003	K-3	*What! Cried Granny: An Almost Bedtime Story* by Kate Lum. Adrian Johnson, ill.

WYOMING

Indian Paintbrush Book Award
1986 <www.ccpls.org/html/indianphtml>
and <www.wyla.org/paintbrush/index.shtml>
4-6

SPONSOR: Wyoming Library Association, Wyoming State Reading Council

PURPOSE: To help Wyoming students in grades four through six become acquainted with the best contemporary authors; become aware of the qualities that make a good book; set a goal to read at least three good books; and to honor an author whose books Wyoming students have enjoyed.

NAME ORIGIN: Named after the state flower—Indian Paintbrush.

VOTING: Students must read a minimum of three books to be eligible to vote.

1986	4-6	*Naya Nuki: Shoshoni Girl Who Ran* by Kenneth Thomasma
1987	4-6	*Hot and Cold Summer* by Johanna Hurwitz
1988	4-6	*The Dollhouse Murders* by Betty Ren Wright
1989	4-6	*The Return of the Indian* by Lynne Reid Banks
1990	4-6	*There's a Boy in the Girls' Bathroom* by Louis Sachar
1991	4-6	*Matilda* by Roald Dahl
1992	4-6	*Maniac Magee* by Jerry Spinelli
1993	4-6	*Pathki Nana: Kootenai Girl Solves a Mystery* by Kenneth Thomasma
1994	4-6	*Shiloh* by Phyllis Reynolds Naylor
1995	4-6	*Rescue Josh McGuire* by Ben Mikaelsen
1996	4-6	*Moho Wat: A Sheepeater Boy Attempts a Rescue* by Kenneth Thomasma
1997	4-6	*Watchdog and the Coyotes* by Bill Wallace
1998	4-6	*Crash* by Jerry Spinelli
1999	4-6	*Saving Shiloh* by Phyllis Reynolds Naylor
2000	4-6	*Harry Potter and the Sorcerer's Stone* by J. K. Rowling
2001	4-6	*Holes* by Louis Sachar
2002	4-6	*Harry Potter and the Goblet of Fire* by J. K. Rowling
2003	4-6	*Among the Hidden* by Margaret Peterson Haddix

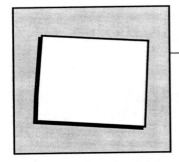

WYOMING

Soaring Eagle Book Award

1989 <www.ccpls.org/html/soaringeagle.
html> and <www.wyla.org/soaringeagle/
index.shtml> 7-12

SPONSOR: Wyoming Library Association, Wyoming State Reading Council

PURPOSE: To help Wyoming students in grades seven through twelve
become acquainted with the best contemporary authors; become aware
of the qualities that make a good book; choose the best rather than the
mediocre; set a goal to read at least three good books; and to honor an
author whose books Wyoming students have enjoyed.

SELECTION CRITERIA: Books may be fiction or nonfiction; must be in
print; the copyright date must be at least four years prior to the award year;
must not have appeared first as a movie or TV show; need not have been
written exclusively for young adults.

VOTING: Students must read a minimum of three books to be eligible to vote.

1989	7-9	*Superfudge* by Judy Blume
1990	7-9	*Someone Is Hiding on Alcatraz Island* by Eve Bunting
	10-12	*Of Love and Shadows* by Isabel Allende
1991	7-9	*Trapped in Death Cave* by Bill Wallace
	10-12	*Princess Ashley* by Richard Peck
1992	7-12	*Dances With Wolves* by Michael Blake
1993	7-12	*Hugh Glass, Mountain Man* by Robert M. McClung
1994	7-12	*Desperate Pursuit* by Gloria Miklowitz
1995	7-12	*Jurassic Park* by Michael Crichton
1996	7-12	*Whispers From the Dead* by Joan Lowery Nixon
1997	7-12	*Hatchet* by Gary Paulsen
1998	7-12	*Freak the Mighty* by Rodman Philbrick
1999	7-12	*Chicken Soup for the Teenage Soul: 101 Stories of Life, Love and Learning*
2000	7-12	*A Child Called "It": One Child's Courage to Survive* by Dave Pelzer
2001	7-12	*She Said Yes: The Unlikely Martyrdom of Cassie Bernall* by Misty Bernall
2002	7-12	*Harry Potter and the Prisoner of Azkaban* by J. K. Rowling
2003	7-12	*Holes* by Louis Sachar

Appendix

Chronological Listing of Awards

DATE	STATE	AWARD
1940	Pacific Northwest	Young Reader's Choice Award
1953	Kansas	William Allen White Children's Book Award
1957	Vermont	Dorothy Canfield Fisher Children's Book Award
1959	Oklahoma	Sequoyah Book Awards
1964	Hawaii	The Nene Award
1969	Georgia	Georgia Children's Literature Book Award
1971	Arkansas	Charlie May Simon Children's Book Award
1972	Missouri	Mark Twain Award
1974	Wisconsin	Golden Archer Award
1975	Indiana	Young Hoosier Book Award
1976	South Carolina	South Carolina Association of School Librarians' Book Award
1976	Massachusetts	Massachusetts Children's Book Award
1976	Colorado	Colorado Children's Book Award
1977	New Jersey	Garden State Children's Book Award
1977	Arizona	Arizona Young Readers' Award
1978	North Dakota	Flicker Tale Children's Book Award
1979	Tennessee	Volunteer State Book Award
1980	Utah	Beehive Awards
1980	New Hampshire	Great Stone Face Award
1980	Minnesota	Maud Hart Lovelace Book Award
1980	Iowa	Iowa Children's Choice Award
1981	Texas	Texas Bluebonnet Award
1981	New Mexico	Land of Enchantment Book Award
1981	Nebraska	Golden Sower Award
1981	Alabama	Emphasis on Reading—Alabama's Children's Choice Award
1982	Washington	Washington Children's Choice Picture Book Award
1982	Virginia	Virginia Young Readers Award
1982	Ohio	Buckeye Children's Book Award
1983	Kentucky	Kentucky Bluegrass Award
1984	Florida	Sunshine State Young Reader's Award
1985	West Virginia	West Virginia Children's Book Award
1985	Iowa	Iowa Teen Award

1985	Colorado	Colorado Blue Spruce Young Adult Book Award
1986	Wyoming	Indian Paintbrush Book Award
1987	South Dakota	Prairie Pasque Award
1988	Nevada	Nevada Young Readers' Award
1988	Maryland	Maryland Children's Book Award
1988	Illinois	Rebecca Caudill Young Readers' Book Award
1989	Wyoming	Soaring Eagle Book Award
1989	Mississippi	Mississippi Children's Book Award
1989	Michigan	Great Lakes' Great Books Award
1989	Florida	Florida Children's Book Award
1990	New York	Charlotte Award
1991	Washington	Evergreen Young Adult Book Award
1991	Rhode Island	Rhode Island Children's Book Award
1991	Montana	Treasure State Award
1991	Maine	Maine Student Book Award
1991	Delaware	Delaware Diamonds Primary Award
1992	Pennsylvania	Pennsylvania Young Reader's Choice Award
1992	North Carolina	North Carolina Children's Book Award
1992	Maryland	Maryland Black-Eyed Susan Book Award
1993	Connecticut	Nutmeg Children's Book Award
1995	New Jersey	Garden State Teen Book Award
1995	Missouri	Show Me Readers Award
1996	Indiana	Eliot Rosewater Indiana High School Book Award
1996	Delaware	Blue Hen Book Award
1996	California	California Young Reader Medal
1997	Vermont	Red Clover Award, Vermont's Children's Choice Picture Book Award
1998	Washington	Sasquatch Reading Award
1998	South Dakota	Prairie Bud Award
1998	Oregon	Patricia Gallagher Picture Book Award
1999	Arkansas	Arkansas Diamond Primary Book Award
1999	Wyoming	Buckaroo Book Award
2000	Louisiana	Louisiana Young Readers' Choice Award
2001	Rhode Island	Rhode Island Teen Book Award
2001	Missouri	Gateway Award
2003	Oregon	Beverly Cleary Children's Choice Award
2004	Iowa	Iowa High School Book Award
2005	Illinois	Monarch Award
2005	Illinois	Abraham Lincoln Illinois High School Book Award

Selected Bibliography

Arth, Joan R. "State Children's Choice Literacy Award Programs: A Research Paper Presented to the Department of Library Science and Information Services." Warrensburg, MO: Central Missouri State University, 1990.

- This study reports on children's choice awards from 1979-89. Data is analyzed to see which authors and books were chosen and what criteria and guidelines were used.

Berman, Matt, and Marigny J. Dupuy. *Children's Book Award Annual.* Englewood, CO: Libraries Unlimited, 1998.

- Covers major national awards, such as the Newbery and Caldecott awards as well as notable and blue ribbon books. Children's choice books are not included. Each book is annotated, with notations of the awards it has won.

Bodart, Joni. *Booktalking the Award Winners: Young Adult Retrospective Volume.* NY: H.W. Wilson, 1996.

- Bodart has written many volumes on the art of booktalking. This one gives tips for booktalking young adult literature.

Bromann, Jennifer. *Booktalking That Works.* NY: Neal-Schuman, 2001.

- A good source for beginners to booktalking, this book also includes research on teen reading habits.

Children's Books: Awards & Prizes: Includes Prizes and Awards for Young Adult Books. NY: Children's Book Council, 1996.

- A compilation of information about children's choice awards as well as other prizes and awards for children's books.

Count on Reading Handbook: Tips for Planning Reading Motivation Programs. Chicago: AASL, 1997.

- This handbook explains the successful "Count on Reading" program in the Colorado Rockies, as well as programs in three other states. It also highlights some of the research on reading programs and gives practical ideas from the Indiana REAP program.

Cox, Ruth E. *Tantalizing Tidbits for Teens: Quick Booktalks for the Busy Library Media Specialist.* Worthington, OH: Linworth, 1994.

- Intriguing one-to-two minute booktalks on 150 books suitable for grades nine through twelve.

Druse, Judy. *Booktalking Tips from A to Z*. Mabee Library, Washburn University. 16 February 2004 <www.washburn.edu/mabee/crc/booktalks/booktalktips.html>

- There are 26 tips for booktalking plus a how-to booktalk page and a listing of sample booktalks.

Jacobsohn, Rachel W. *The Reading Group Handbook: Everything You Need to Know, From Choosing Members to Leading Discussions*. NY: Hyperion, 1994.

- A primer on how to start a book discussion group.

Jay, M. Ellen, and Hilda L. Jay. *Ready-to-Go Reading Incentives for Schools and Libraries*. NY: Neal-Schuman, 1998.

- Ideas for reading incentive programs abound in this book, along with recordkeeping forms to keep track of what has been read by the students.

Jones, Delores Blyth. *Children's Literature Awards and Winners: A Directory of Prizes, Authors, and Illustrators*, third edition. Detroit: Gale, 1994.

- Children's choice awards, as well as many other children book awards are described, accompanied by yearly lists of the winning titles.

Keane, Nancy. *Booktalking Across the Curriculum: The Middle Years*. Englewood, CO: Libraries Unlimited, 2003.

- A recent collection of 170 booktalks divides the mostly fiction selections into subjects across the curriculum. Ranging from mathematics and science to U.S. and world history, the reading levels are for grades three through eight. A good compilation of titles especially for middle school curriculum.

Nancy Keane's Booktalks—Quick and Simple. 16 February 2004 <nancykeane.com/booktalks>

- More than 1,400 ready to use booktalks for children grades seven through twelve can be found at this site. The booktalks are arranged by title, author, interest level, and subject, plus there are pages of FAQs and booktalking tips.

Krashen, Stephen. *The Power of Reading: Insights from the Research*. Englewood, CO: Libraries Unlimited, 1993.

- Studies show that free voluntary reading for pleasure improves reading.

Langemack, Chapple. *The Booktalker's Bible: How to Talk About Books You Love to Any Audience*. Englewood, CO: Libraries Unlimited, 2003.

- Langemack discusses the six golden rules of booktalking, including rule one: read the book! Her suggestions are for booktalking to children, teenagers, or adults. Sample booktalks are included.

Littlejohn, Carol. *Still Talking That Book! Booktalks to Promote Reading Grades 3-12*. Worthington, OH: Linworth, 2003.

- Includes title, author, genre, and subject indexes to 136 new books to help find just the right book to booktalk. This is the fourth edition of Littlejohn's series about booktalking. Her 1999 edition, *Talk That Book! Booktalks to Promote Reading,* is also a good resource.

Rochman, Hazel. *Tales of Love and Terror: Booktalking the Classics, Old and New*. Chicago: ALA, 1987.

- Rochman gives tips with her practical ideas on how to get teenagers to read classic literature.

Works, Robin. *Promoting Reading With Reading Programs*. NY: Neal-Schuman, 1992.

- This book is a practical and helpful planning guide for librarians who need story hour, display, and incentive ideas. It contains fingerplays, bibliographies of books on selected topics, and many suggestions for promoting reading.

Title Index

C

I

J

K

Author/Illustrator Index

A

Aardema, Verna 152
Adler, Carole S. 64
Adler, David 33,67,96,121
Ahlberg, Allan . . . .
27,42
Ahlberg, Janet 27,42
Alborough, Jez 135
Alexander, Martha 66
Aliki 95,96
Allard, Harry 27,36,46,88,107
Allen, Jonathan 25,142,146
Allen, Judy 147
Allende, Isabel 156
Almond, David 99
Alphin, Elaine 142
Ames, Lee J. 95
Ancona, George 25
Anderson, Laurie Halse 54,67,77,
99,112,125,131,144
Anderson, Margaret . . . . .J 31
Anson, Jay 124
Archambault, John 66
Armstrong, William 48,82
Arnold, Elliott 63
Arnold, Marsha Diane . . . .
57,84,147
Arnold, Tedd 24,37,42,46,
105,107,119,130
Arrick, Fran 124
Atkin, S. Beth 25
Atwater, Florence 116
Atwater, Richard 116
Auch, Mary Jane 103,107,152
Avi 28,44,73,98,101,
102,121,135,136,142,144

B

Bach, Richard 48
Bachrach, Susan D. 102
Bailey, Jean 63
Baker, Barbara 96
Balian, Lorna 24,36,45,151
Ball, Zachary [pseud.] 64,138
Ballard, Robert 142
Banks, Lynne Reid 27,53,74,
76,91,92,117,142,155

Barrett, Judi 36,40,46,88
Barrett, Ron, ill. 36,40,46,88
Barron, T.A 135
Base, Graeme 28
Bauer, Joan 118
Bauer, Marion Dane 64,107,152
Bedard, Michael 136
Bell, Thelma Harrington 138
Bellairs, John 134,141
Bennett, Cherie 99
Benson, Patrick, ill. 102
Berenstain, Jan 108
Berenstain, Stan 108
Bernall, Misty 156
Bernhard, Durga, ill. 86
Bernhard, Emery 86
Berry, Liz 143
Bickel, Cindy 136
Bildner, Phil 133
Birdseye, Tom 71,84,88,147
Bitton-Jackson, Livia 111
Black, Irma Simonton 24
Blake, Michael 156
Blake, Robert J. .58,86,88,140,143,147
Bloor, Edward 73,76,79,91,99,125
Blume, Judy 24,27,30,34,
36,43,44,45,46,48,49,56,59,60,62,69,
70,74,76,88,90,92,95,100,106,107,
108,111,117,119,123,129,130,132,
134,138,141,151,156
Blundell, Tony 142
Bond, Felicia, ill. 24,37,46,90,108
Brashares, Ann 4,71,112,122
Brett, Jan 70,86
Brittain, Bill 30,38,91
Brown, Marc 23,37,96
Brown, Margaret Wise 23
Brown, Ruth 142
Bruchac, Joseph 107,112,121
Brunkus, Denise, ill. 28
Buchanan, William J. 124
Budbill, David 138
Buehner, Caralyn 135
Buehner, Mark, ill. 28,39,57,67,
70,91,135,147
Bulla, Clyde Robert 30,111,124
Bunting, Eve 25,43,44,49,82,
88,111,118,119,124,130,135,142,143,
149,156

Y

Z